MATT HARTLEY

Matt Hartley grew up in the Peak District and studied Drama at the University of Hull. Matt's first play *Sixty Five Miles* won a Bruntwood Award in the inaugural Bruntwood Prize for Playwriting and was produced by Paines Plough/Hull Truck. Other work for theatre includes *Myth* (Royal Shakespeare Company); *Here I Belong* (Pentabus); *Horizon* (National Theatre Connections); *Microcosm* (Soho); *The Bee* (Edinburgh Festival); *Punch* (Hampstead/Heat & Light Company); *Epic*, *Trolls*, *Life for Beginners* (Theatre503). Radio credits include *The Pursuit*, *Final Call* (Radio 4). Matt is currently under commission to the Hampstead Theatre, Royal Shakespeare Company and West Yorkshire Playhouse. *Here I Belong* will be revived by Pentabus in spring 2018.

Matt Hartley

DEPOSIT

NICK HERN BOOKS

London

www.nickhernbooks.co.uk

A Nick Hern Book

Deposit first published in Great Britain as a paperback original in 2015 by Nick Hern Books Limited, The Glasshouse, 49a Goldhawk Road, London W12 8QP

This new edition published 2017

Deposit copyright © 2015, 2017 Matt Hartley

Matt Hartley has asserted his right to be identified as the author of this work

Cover design: SWD

Designed and typeset by Nick Hern Books, London
Printed in the UK by Mimeo Ltd, Huntingdon, Cambridgeshire PE29 6XX

A CIP catalogue record for this book is available from the British Library

ISBN 978 1 84842 678 8

Deposit was first performed at Hampstead Theatre Downstairs, London, on 12 March 2015. The cast was as follows:

BEN	Ben Addis
RACHEL	Akiya Henry
SAM	Jack Monaghan
MELANIE	Laura Morgan

Director	Lisa Spirling
Designer	Polly Sullivan
Lighting	Johanna Town
Sound	Richard Hammarton
Movement Director	John Ross
Assistant Director	Jamie Billings
Stage Manager	Hannah Harte

The play was revived at Hampstead Theatre Downstairs, London, on 17 May 2017 (previews from 11 May). The cast was as follows:

BEN	Ben Addis
SAM	Karl Davies
RACHEL	Natalie Dew
MELANIE	Nicola Kavanagh

Director	Lisa Spirling
Designer	Polly Sullivan
Lighting Designer	Johanna Town
Sound Designer	Richard Hammarton
Movement Director	John Ross
Assistant Director	Emily Aboud
Associate Lighting Designer	Rory Beaton
Associate Movement Director	Chi-San Howard
Production Manager	Pip Robinson
Stage Manager	Sophie Sierra
Assistant Stage Manager	Paige Harris
Costume Supervisor	Holly Henshaw

Acknowledgements

I would like to thank the following people for their support, inspiration and belief in this project:

Ed and Greg, and all the fantastic staff at the Hampstead Theatre. Severine Magois for the grammar checking. Giles Smart and Jen Thomas at United Agents. And all at Nick Hern Books for so generously publishing this version.

The following actors who were so generous in its development: Chris Brandon, Graham Butler, Ben Dilloway, Becci Gemmill, David Hartley, Akiya Henry, Jack Monaghan, Laura Morgan, Jenny Rainsford, and Ashley Zhangazha.

The brilliant creative and technical team that have (once again) been assembled, who have helped me to see the world less literally. And to the wonderful actors: Ben Addis, Karl Davies, Natalie Dew and Nicola Kavanagh for bringing it to life every night.

All those that I have ever lived with, for better or worse, who have provided unwitting inspiration. And of course everyone else to whom certain incidents may resonate.

And a huge heartfelt thanks to Will Mortimer and Lisa Spirling. Two of my oldest champions, who pushed and pushed and made it happen.

M.H.

For Eden and Pez:
for making the move so easy.

Characters

RACHEL MAGUIRE, *thirty-two, primary schoolteacher. 28K.*
BEN EDWARDS, *thirty-four, press officer. 29.5K.*
MELANIE CRAWFORD, *thirty-two, marketing officer. 40K.*
SAM GRANT, *twenty-nine, doctor. 45K (speciality grade).*

A forward slash (/) at the end of a line indicates continued speech.

Setting

A very, very small one-bedroom attic flat in a terraced house. Herne Hill, London. The flat consists of a bedroom, just big enough for a double bed. Adjoining it is a living room, slightly bigger, with no door. Off the corridor is a tiny kitchen and separate bathroom. But none of this has to be imagined realistically. The set should feel like a cage, a prison, a UFC fighting ring, a zoo enclosure. Throughout the play, the space that the flat is imagined in should shrink until it barely exists.

November 2015 – November 2016.

This text went to press before the end of rehearsals and so may differ slightly from the play as performed.

November

The sun rises on BEN *and* RACHEL. *They are happy, content, in a space that is their own.*

Suddenly this ends as… RACHEL *welcomes* MELANIE *into the flat.*

MELANIE *is carrying a bottle of Prosecco and breathing heavily.* BEN *waits in the 'living room', four glasses of Prosecco at the ready.*

MELANIE. Hello!!!

RACHEL. Hiya! Welcome! Oh god, are you alright, Mel?

MELANIE. I need to get my breath back, all those stairs. I won't be needing my gym membership any more!

MELANIE *hugs* RACHEL.

Hello!

RACHEL. Hi. Where's Sam?

MELANIE. He's just bringing a few things up.

RACHEL. Does he need a hand?

MELANIE. No, no, it's good for him. Needs building up. Oh my god, I can't believe this!

RACHEL. I know.

MELANIE. Me and you, back under one roof, living together. So exciting!!

RACHEL. We're assembled in your room.

MELANIE. 'Your' room. Ahhhh! Sounds just like halls.

They enter the room.

There he is. Roomie Number Two!

BEN. Indeed. Hi, Mel.

They share a welcome embrace.

A welcome drink?

He passes MELANIE *a glass and takes the bottle from her.*

MELANIE. Uh-oh. My poor liver. Is this what the year ahead looks like?!

RACHEL. Imagine!

MELANIE *surveys the scene.*

MELANIE. So this is it: Home.

BEN. It is, yeah.

Loud crashing from the corridor. SAM *has entered. He is overloaded with bags.*

MELANIE. Sam?

SAM. Nothing's broken.

MELANIE. Might as well bring everything through here.

BEN *steps out into the corridor.*

BEN. Jeez, is this everything you own?

SAM. Virtually.

MELANIE. I thought it was best to do it all in one go.

SAM. Can I put them down?

MELANIE. Well yes, this is where we live now, silly.

He dumps them down.

RACHEL. Hi, Sam.

SAM. Hi.

RACHEL. Are you okay?

SAM. Yes. You?

RACHEL. Yes.

BEN. Mate.

SAM. Ben.

BEN. Welcome.

SAM. Thanks. This is it then?

BEN. Yes.

SAM. This is our room?

MELANIE. Yes!

BEN. It's not Buckingham Palace.

SAM. No. No, it's not.

MELANIE. It's great. Nice view.

RACHEL. Oh yes. If you bend, peer out, you can see The Shard.

MELANIE. Oh wow. Hear that, Sam?

SAM. Yes.

MELANIE. The Shard!

SAM. Yes.

MELANIE *tries to look for it.*

MELANIE. Hmmm… I can't…

RACHEL. Bit more to the right…

MELANIE. Not…

RACHEL. If you lean a bit further. That flashing, see the
flashing light?

MELANIE. Yes. Yes. I see it, I can see the point! The little
light at the top. Amazing! Sam, Sam, come and look! The
Shard! Sam?

SAM. There's no bed.

RACHEL. No, sorry, it's a sofa bed. Very comfy though. Folds
down. Takes no time at all.

BEN. We did tell you that, didn't we?

MELANIE. Yes, yes, you did.

SAM. I think it's just actually seeing it.

MELANIE. It's fine. I've totally slept on worse things!

SAM. Odd position.

RACHEL. We just tried out a few things…

BEN. Layout-wise. Feel free to move and alter, it's completely your choice.

SAM. I'd put it there.

BEN. We tried that, we liked it –

SAM. Or at least against the wall. It's an obstacle at the moment. We'd have to keep walking round. Help me out, Ben.

BEN. What?

SAM. The sofa.

BEN. Don't you want a drink or a tour first?

MELANIE. You better give him a hand, he won't be able to concentrate on anything else until it's done.

SAM. That's true.

BEN. Okay. Sure.

They move the sofa.

SAM. Yes. Better. Fantastic.

RACHEL. Well, welcome!

MELANIE. Thank you!

SAM. Or should we say 'Welcome'. You are in our room after all.

RACHEL. Of course, yes, sorry. Thank you.

BEN. Yes, thank you for your hospitality.

SAM. It's our pleasure.

BEN *offers a drink to* SAM.

Oh no, not for me.

BEN. No?

SAM. No.

BEN. Not telling me you've gone teetotal, are you? I was
    looking forward to replicating our night out at Freud's!

SAM. Fear not, we can get completely Winehoused again.

MELANIE. Sam!

SAM. Not appropriate?

MELANIE. No.

SAM. I'm just likely to be operating on a child in a few hours.

MELANIE. Hear that?

RACHEL. Yes.

MELANIE. A child!

RACHEL. Yes.

MELANIE. He's so good, isn't he!

> MELANIE *kisses* SAM. *The kiss lasts a little longer than*
> BEN *and* RACHEL *feel comfortable with.* MELANIE *and*
> SAM *stop.*

> Uh-oh, get a room, eh. Or out of it should I say!

BEN. Is now a good time to tell you there's no door?

> *Smiles all round.*

SAM. We will get a screen.

MELANIE. Yes. And until then if it sounds like sex, it probably
    will be sex, so don't feel the need to stick your nose in and
    check. I learnt the hard way with you and Chris Potter, didn't
    I, Rach!

RACHEL. I never said come in!

MELANIE. Sounded very similar. Such an eyeful. Literally.

BEN. Yeah, we all have our embarrassing stories, don't we, Mel?

MELANIE. Oh my god, I am so giddy, this is going to be so much fun, isn't it! So do we get a tour, then?

RACHEL. Yes, sorry, of course.

MELANIE. Check out our home. Hear that, Sam?!

SAM. Yes.

MELANIE. Home!

SAM. Yes.

BEN. Pack your Kendal Mint Cake, this is a serious expedition.

RACHEL. So, yes, if you'd like to follow me.

> BEN *remains in the living room as* RACHEL *conducts a brief tour. During the tour he tops his drink up, drinks some more, tops it up again.*

Well, first up is mine and Ben's room.

MELANIE. Right. Lovely. Okay. Really sweet. Cosy.

RACHEL. Yeah, we're trying to use words like that.

MELANIE. You've got built-in wardrobes, hide everything away. That is heaven sent.

SAM. If you turned the bed ninety degrees you would have more floor space.

RACHEL. Well, that's something to think about.

SAM. I'm interfering, aren't I.

> MELANIE *sits on the bed.*

MELANIE. Uh-oh! Caution, this bed's a rattler. I hope you've taken that into consideration.

BEN. You can stop there, Mel.

MELANIE. Was he talking to me?

BEN. Yes, I can hear you.

MELANIE. Wow, from in there, really is –

BEN. Cosy?

MELANIE. Exactly, yes.

BEN. Yes. Moving on, this is the bathroom.

MELANIE. Oh, commanding! After you.

RACHEL. I know the whole thing needs a bit of love, but the shower's very powerful, the water comes out hot, and the toilet flushes.

SAM. You'd hope it would for fourteen hundred a month.

RACHEL. Yeah, yes you would. Did you just give me a thumbs-up?

MELANIE. I did! Where's next?

BEN. West wing.

MELANIE. West wing! You hear that, Sam?

SAM. Yes.

MELANIE. West wing.

SAM. Yes.

MELANIE. The west wing. Hilarious!

RACHEL *walks down the corridor. Squeezes by* SAM.

RACHEL. Sorry, can I just squeeze by.

MELANIE. Uh-oh, gridlock!!

RACHEL. Yeah, beep, beep. Thank you. Kitchen. Again, it's –

MELANIE. Compact.

RACHEL. Yes, but there are lots of cupboards. Really maximised the space.

MELANIE. Oh yes, very well designed.

RACHEL. I think so.

BEN. I think they would have probably knocked this wall down, but it's –

SAM. Load-bearing.

BEN. Yes, exactly. Load-bearing.

MELANIE. Have you really only been here two nights? It feels so lived in.

SAM. Yes, it does.

RACHEL. Sorry, please do move things, nothing is set in stone.

BEN. Just plates and pans.

SAM. Ow.

RACHEL. Oh god, sorry, did I just tread on your toe, Sam?

SAM. It's fine.

RACHEL. Sorry. Well, that sort of concludes the tour. So what do you think, is this going to be alright?

MELANIE. Yeah, yeah, of course.

RACHEL. Really?

MELANIE. Yeaaahhhhh!

BEN. This is a palace compared to what else we viewed.

RACHEL. Really is.

BEN. Not a chance in hell of a two-bed for the price we all agreed. The ones that were perhaps slightly nicer, they had a living-kitchen combo, which wouldn't have worked.

MELANIE. I know, we know, you're not the only ones that looked.

SAM. I couldn't even get an appointment to view most properties.

MELANIE. You did the right thing. Didn't they?!

SAM. Yes.

RACHEL. Are you sure?

SAM. If my face is telling a different story it's because I'm exhausted. This rota I am on seems never ending.

MELANIE. He's being worked so hard, aren't you.

SAM. I am, yes. I'm constantly exhausted.

RACHEL. So that sofa is really the last thing you wanted to see. Sorry.

SAM. It's not ideal. But there are bigger things at stake. And I can sleep in a year's time when I have my own bed, in my, our, own home.

MELANIE. Exactly. Keywords. Own. Home. Did you hear that?

RACHEL. Yes.

MELANIE. Own home!

RACHEL. Yes.

MELANIE. Oh the thought!!

RACHEL. I know.

They step back into the living room. Topping up their drinks as they do.

If you want, just to throw this out there, we can swap rooms, at halfway, to even the experience up.

BEN *mouths 'What are you doing?' to* RACHEL.

MELANIE. You don't have to say that.

RACHEL. I do.

BEN *mouths 'No, you don't' to* RACHEL.

SAM. That's very kind.

MELANIE. But not necessary. And anyway, this is slightly bigger and we can totally see The Shard. Well... sort of... Seriously, put that thought out of your mind. You did the hard work finding this place.

BEN *nods in agreement.*

RACHEL. The offer's there. We can review it –

BEN. But without, I don't want to sound ominous, but you know that the estate agents, landlord, have no idea about you, officially you don't live here, so it makes sense that it starts off this way round.

RACHEL. And so, sorry, with that in mind, you might have to do things like: put the bed back to being a sofa, stuff away, et cetera, if they came to check.

MELANIE. Hear that?

SAM. Yes.

MELANIE. We're stowaways.

SAM. Yes.

MELANIE. How exciting.

SAM. Anne Frank.

MELANIE. Sam!

SAM. That was inappropriate, wasn't it.

MELANIE. Yes, Sam.

BEN. I'm not mad keen on estate agents but I think they're perhaps slightly less evil than Nazis.

RACHEL. You weren't saying that when you saw the fee breakdown. One hundred and seventy-five pounds administration –

BEN. It's mental, didn't even show us round, all he did was open the door.

MELANIE. Er, vile.

SAM. It's a racket.

BEN. Really is.

RACHEL. It gets worse. Sorry. They charged the same for referencing. And one hundred for an inventory.

BEN. Like how on earth? Why do we pay for that and not the landlord?

RACHEL. We paid it. We had no choice. Someone would have.

SAM. Do we need to contribute towards that?

RACHEL. Sorry, yes. Well, half of it to be precise.

SAM. Of course. Shall we get it all out of the way? The money.

MELANIE. Cheers, Sam, take the gloss off the fizz, why don't you!

BEN. Actually, it would help our bank account from looking so massively depressed.

MELANIE. Of course, yes. We're all in the same boat here.

SAM. If you write down a breakdown and the amount, I will action it.

RACHEL. I have actually written it down. A little contract.

MELANIE. Contract?

RACHEL. Nothing official obviously, not legally binding, but friendship-binding. Sorry, does that seem aggressive?

MELANIE. No, no, we know you're /

RACHEL. It's a habit.

MELANIE. / meticulous. I love that, we love that about you, don't we?

SAM. Yes.

RACHEL. Thanks. I think all the timetables and lesson plans I have to do /

MELANIE. Oh, hear that, Sam?

SAM. Yes.

MELANIE. Lesson plans.

SAM. Yes.

MELANIE. Adorable!

RACHEL. / this was just another. I'll stop talking about it. Sorry. Here.

RACHEL *has handed over a piece of paper.*

MELANIE. Oh, formal.

RACHEL. I know, sorry.

MELANIE. We Rachel Maguire, Ben Edwards, Melanie Crawford and Dr Sam Grant agree to co-habit for the period of one year in Flat 3, 7 Kestrel Avenue. We will equally divide rent and bills, which are listed below. Sam?

SAM *looks at the figures.*

SAM. Eighteen hundred and forty-two pounds a month.

RACHEL. When we sat down and did this, we realised that if it was just the two of us doing this, by the time we'd paid for everything, we'd only have about three hundred pounds each to live on a month. Be impossible to save enough, / but not any more!

MELANIE. Wow. Oh really? That's all you have left? Right.

RACHEL. I've been tough on myself, I've cut out my morning coffee.

MELANIE. Well, it adds up, one a day suddenly you're spending twenty pounds a week on them.

SAM. Over a thousand pounds a year.

RACHEL. Exactly. And that's a tenth of what we're hoping to save this year.

MELANIE. Oh right, ten?

RACHEL. Yeah. Is that not as much, does that not sound much…?

SAM. We see this year as the year of the compromise.

MELANIE. Exactly that. Year of the compromise. I cut up my Whistles store card. But that doesn't mean it has to be all doom and boohoo gloom does it.

RACHEL. God, no. It's a chapter in our lives.

MELANIE. Exactly! A chapter. I love it. So profound.

BEN. Shall we sign this?

MELANIE. Sign? Of course, yes.

They start to sign.

BEN. Should take a photo of this moment as well.

MELANIE. Totally.

BEN. I was joking.

MELANIE. No, get in. Seriously. Mark this moment forever.

They gather in front of MELANIE*'s camera as* BEN *tries to make a speech.*

BEN. Well, today is a brave day, friends are uniting. To help each other's dreams come true. And yes, we will lie to estate agents, landlords –

SAM. And power companies.

BEN. Yes, and bloody power companies /

MELANIE takes a selfie with them holding the contract. As BEN *continues his speech.*

MELANIE. Say…?

RACHEL. Deposit?

MELANIE. Yeah that's a good one.

They say 'Deposit'. MELANIE *checks.*

Oh god that's awful. One more. Say something different. Something fun. I know: 'Roomies'.

BEN. / but we don't care about them. After all they are the arseholes who have put us in this position to start with. From this day forward we are on the march. That march towards our goal. A bit of land. A roof to call our own. Where we'll be free of landlords and –

RACHEL *and* MELANIE. Roomies.

They raise glasses. They toast. They drink.

Time passes. The flat becomes lived in. They cross paths in the corridor. They pop into each other's room. They drink. They cook for each other. They kiss and cuddle. They laugh.

December

BEN *has just returned from work, he is in the doorway, a bag by his feet.* SAM, RACHEL *and* MELANIE *are singing 'Happy Birthday' to him.*

BEN. Thank you.

> *They continue.*

> Yep. Okay. Thanks.

> *Still not finished.*

> Very kind.

> *Not quite finished.*

> Angels, all of you.

> *They finish.*

> Thank you. That was really, truly delightful…

> MELANIE *starts to sing 'For He's a Jolly Good Fellow'.*

> Great, yes, thanks, really –

MELANIE. Surprise!!

BEN. Indeed, yes. Truly is a surprise. I didn't think you even knew.

MELANIE. Hear that?

RACHEL. Yes.

MELANIE. Didn't think we knew!

RACHEL. Yes.

MELANIE. Of course we knew! Thirty-five, how could we forget that!!

SAM. What a milestone.

BEN. Yes, yes, a real milestone.

SAM. Very exciting.

BEN. Oh yes, I'm very old now, very very old. Surprised I even made it up the stairs.

MELANIE. Listen to him, so dramatic, god, some of us aren't that far behind you, you know. Well, obviously not the toy boy. Hear that.

SAM. Yes.

MELANIE. Toy boy.

SAM. Yes.

MELANIE. I'm such a cradle-snatcher!

SAM. I'm actually very jealous, Ben. I can't wait to be thirty-five.

BEN. I think I said that when I was twenty-nine as well.

SAM. Consulting. A home. Solidification and potential expansion of this pairing.

MELANIE. Oh god, he knows how to warm my ovaries up.

RACHEL. Happy birthday!

BEN. Is this your doing?

MELANIE. Don't go taking all the credit, Rach!

RACHEL. Sorry, I know you didn't want a party or any fuss, but we couldn't not have a little celebration.

MELANIE. God, no.

RACHEL. It's your birthday, Ben.

SAM *offers* BEN *a bottle of El Jimador, Silver.*

SAM. Here.

BEN. Oh, wow, you got –

SAM. I know it's your favourite.

MELANIE. Now come through into the party room.

They lead BEN *into the living room.*

RACHEL. Very exclusive.

MELANIE. Here you will find the dance floor.

BEN. Let me put my bag away first.

MELANIE. No, no, it's your bloody birthday, you just sit, relax, we'll take care of everything for you. Sam will take your bag.

BEN. You really didn't have to do this.

MELANIE. We did.

BEN. Other people aren't coming here, are they?

RACHEL. Here, god no! We wouldn't do that.

MELANIE. Just the four of us!

RACHEL. We've got all your favourite things.

MELANIE. Playlist of your dreams. Docked and ready.

RACHEL. All you have to do is press play.

BEN. Well, I must say this is really not what I was expecting, I thought –

MELANIE. Nope, no talking, drinking and dancing, that is all. You hear?

BEN. Yes.

MELANIE. Drinking and dancing!

BEN. Yes.

RACHEL. We all need to see the wolf.

MELANIE. Yes, yes, the wolf!

BEN. He's not been out in years.

RACHEL. Well then release him.

BEN. Are you prepared for that?

RACHEL. I want to see him howl at the moon.

BEN. Are you pressing play or do I have to get my own birthday party started?

MELANIE. That is what I wanted to hear!

Music starts.

RACHEL. Sorry.

BEN. Absolutely no need.

   SAM *returns*.

   Are you able to drink tonight?

SAM. I am.

BEN. No children to operate on?

SAM. Plenty. I'm going to be the next Shipman.

MELANIE. Sam!

SAM. Too far?

MELANIE. Yes, Sam, too far.

SAM. I arranged my shifts to allow me to imbibe.

BEN. Good man.

MELANIE. Er, why are you not dancing?

BEN. Be afraid, it is about to begin.

   And it does.

   They dance.

   They drink.

   BEN *ends up dancing like a wolf.*

   They smile and laugh and encourage each other.

   MELANIE *and* RACHEL *have a dance-off.*

   They encourage SAM *to dance.*

   He ends up dancing.

   He is highly impressive.

   They applaud.

   They continue dancing.

   They slowly start to stop.

   Apart from BEN *who keeps dancing and dancing and dancing.*

   I'm thirty-five!

ALL. Yes!

BEN. Thirty-five. I'm thirty-five! Thirty-five!! Thirty-five years old!!! Thirty-five years old... Thirty-five.

RACHEL. Ben?

BEN. I'm thirty-five years old!!!

RACHEL. Heh heh.

BEN.... Thirty-five.

   MELANIE *turns the stereo off.*

   Turn that back on.

RACHEL. Let's get you to bed.

MELANIE. I think we all know it's time to say goodnight.

BEN. No, no, no, it's not that time. I'm not ready. How many times do you think I'm thirty-five?! Put it back on. Put it back on!

   MELANIE *does.*

   Yeah!!!

   BEN *dances.*

   Thirty-five, Rach!

RACHEL. Yeah.

BEN. Thirty-five!!

   BEN *stops. He looks around, in disbelief at how he's living.*

   Thirty-five.

RACHEL. It's just a number.

BEN. Is it?

RACHEL. Yes.

BEN. Is it?

RACHEL. Yes.

MELANIE. Totally.

BEN. You can turn it off now, Mel.

MELANIE. We can carry on.

BEN. It's okay. I'll go to bed.

MELANIE. Okay.

BEN. Thank you, one and all, thank you –

RACHEL. Come on, time for bed, let Mel and Sam have their room back.

BEN. I still haven't said all I needed to –

RACHEL. They know, they know.

> RACHEL *and* BEN *go into their bedroom.*

BEN. I'm going to be completely upfront, there's absolutely no way I'm going to be able to give you any sort of sexual gratification, right now.

RACHEL. That's okay.

BEN. Is it?

RACHEL. It is, yes.

BEN. I did show you the wolf though, and that I know, that is what made this, this you and I, the wolf brought us together.

RACHEL. Yes, he did.

BEN. Brought us together, together.

MELANIE. Night!

RACHEL. Night!

> BEN *is asleep.*

> RACHEL *lies down next to him.*

> *Hugs him.*

> MELANIE *and* SAM.

MELANIE. You were superb earlier, you hear.

SAM. Yes.

MELANIE. Superb.

SAM. Yes.

MELANIE. Sit there.

> SAM *looks at the corridor.*

Quiet.

> SAM *goes and sits.* MELANIE *approaches.* RACHEL *sits up in bed. She listens as* SAM *and* MELANIE *have sex.*

> *Time passes.*

> *They spend time with each other.* MELANIE *and* RACHEL *bond.* SAM *and* BEN *attempt to bond.* MELANIE *and* RACHEL *spend more time together.* SAM *and* BEN *potter.* SAM *and* BEN *go out.*

January

MELANIE *and* RACHEL *are in the bathroom.* RACHEL *is scrubbing her hands.* MELANIE *has two drinks with her.*

MELANIE. It's a simple mistake: water-proof, acrylic.

RACHEL. Is it?

MELANIE. Completely. Hundred per cent, yes. Paint is paint. Was it on their faces?

RACHEL. Faces, everywhere. It was meant to be a fun end to the day. And yet all I end up getting is 'My child, my child you make look like a clown, like crazy clown, you going to wash this off, you going to do that.' I'm never trusting that TA again. Still can't get it out from under my nails.

MELANIE. Here. Gin.

RACHEL. Thank you.

> RACHEL *dries her hands. Drinks. Goes through to the bedroom.* MELANIE *follows.*

You know that some of the kids will still be covered in it in the morning.

MELANIE. It comes off.

RACHEL. If you have someone to help you wash it off.

MELANIE. Oh, bless them.

RACHEL. Honestly, you know, I have to really check myself sometimes when I think that this scenario, us, is a first-world problem. It's not even a ripple.

MELANIE. Look at you, changing lives.

RACHEL. By poisoning them?

MELANIE. Seriously, you're like the gateway, like these kids yeah, they have to get through you to get to the future. You change people. Hear that?

RACHEL. Alright, alright.

MELANIE. Change people.

RACHEL. Yeah. Maybe.

MELANIE. No maybes. Fact. Polar opposite of me. All I did today. Four meetings, hundreds of emails and all that resulted in was the change of font on a bottle of bleach. Bleach! And that, like, is a day that actually has an end product.

RACHEL. I'm sure it looks fantastic.

MELANIE. That's not really the point, Rach.

RACHEL. Sorry, of course.

MELANIE. Oh my god, have you seen that Claire Anderson has got engaged?

RACHEL. How could I not, it's all over Facebook.

MELANIE. What do you think Ben will say?

RACHEL. That it doesn't interest him in the slightest. It was a long, long time ago.

MELANIE. She broke his heart.

RACHEL. That's a bit OTT.

MELANIE. We all lived through it. Heh, it might push him to buck up his game.

RACHEL. Buck up his game?

MELANIE. Yeah, we all know what she said to him.

RACHEL. And it's still out of order. Ben is ambitious. He is. Sorry, but he's been unlucky recently. He came very close to a promotion. Really close. It's competitive out there.

MELANIE. You're worried, aren't you?

RACHEL. No. No. No. Perhaps. A little. He's got this paranoia about money at the moment. Especially after he heard how much you and Sam were saving.

MELANIE. Sam so shouldn't have said –

RACHEL. Well, we did ask the question. We thought it would be more. I think we were just surprised it was three times as much as us. And turning thirty-five and now if he sees Claire is engaged, they have their own flat, all those things, it might just add to this insecurity.

MELANIE. There are worser things in the world for him to be. It might give him a bit of an incentive, to be active, yeah?

RACHEL. He is –

MELANIE. Oh, come on, I want to shake him for you. He's not the Ben you fell in love with at eighteen.

RACHEL. I have not been in love with Ben since I was eighteen.

MELANIE. Yes, you have. From that first moment you saw him. And who could blame you, even I fancied Ben a little when we first met him. He was so confident. And now he's just…

RACHEL. He is not that noise.

MELANIE. Rach, he can't stay in that job forever, can he? For both your sakes. Oh, come on, you know that's true.

RACHEL. Even if I did think that.

MELANIE. Which you do?

RACHEL. I couldn't say anything.

MELANIE. Er, yes you can. This is a big thing. Your future lives together.

RACHEL. Don't you dare say it.

MELANIE. It's not a poisonous word.

RACHEL. Do you know how many people ask me when's Ben going to propose? I'm, we're, so bored of it.

MELANIE. You'd say yes, though, wouldn't you?

RACHEL. I think the fact that we're buying a home together, locked in debt for eternity, I think that tells you all you need to know.

MELANIE. How's that going, the home-buying?

RACHEL. Great. I'm living with this complete idiot though.

MELANIE. Alright, point taken, I won't bring it up again.

RACHEL. If it happens, it happens, but look around, it's not the priority right now.

MELANIE. I hear you.

RACHEL. Can't all be like Sam.

MELANIE. Like Sam, what?

RACHEL. So certain. Don't think I didn't hear him say what he did on Ben's birthday. About marriage. Babies. You. That's not that long.

MELANIE. You and him are pretty similar, you know. Both love lists. And so yes, that's on the list. He's been very clear about that.

RACHEL. And you're happy with that?

MELANIE. We're buying a home together.

RACHEL. Yes, but is that just what you think you should be doing?

MELANIE. I like the simplicity of it. It's honest. No drama.

RACHEL. Yeah.

MELANIE. I sleep so soundly next to him. I spent so long not sleeping.

RACHEL. Not all the time, though: sleep soundly, next to him. Sorry. I heard you the other night.

MELANIE. You didn't!

RACHEL. Right up to the finish.

MELANIE. You listened?

RACHEL. You didn't give me much choice.

MELANIE. Well, if it's of any comfort, I've not heard you.

RACHEL. Are they my socks?

MELANIE. That bloody clothes rail, nothing ever dries on it. What, do you mind?

RACHEL. Sorry, no, I don't mind. It's completely fine. Completely. They're just socks.

MELANIE. You'll want me to tell you that I've been using your toothbrush next.

RACHEL. You've been using my toothbrush!?

MELANIE. No – I mean. Jesus, we're not at university any more.

RACHEL. You used my toothbrush at uni?!

MELANIE. Like you didn't use mine.

RACHEL. No. Mel, sorry no, I didn't.

MELANIE. Oh. Well if you want you can use mine now, I suppose. Joking, I take my oral health totally seriously now. Let me do your nails.

MELANIE *goes to get a nail file from the living room.*

RACHEL. Has anyone said anything to you about this? About this living arrangement?

MELANIE. Abby thought it was hilarious.

RACHEL. Hilarious?

MELANIE. Oh yeah, she wants to come round. Don't worry, I said she can't. This is not a place for hosting.

RACHEL. And we're not an exhibit either, that's how she'd treat it.

MELANIE. She actually said it was an extremely sensible idea.

RACHEL. That's easy for her to say, isn't it, with that loan her dad gave her. I say loan.

Ah, I've got to stop this. I'm turning every friend into the competition.

BEN *enters the flat.*

BEN. Evening.

MELANIE. Hiya.

MELANIE *goes past* BEN *and back to the bedroom.*

BEN. In a rush?

MELANIE. Rach requires an emergency manicure.

BEN. Oh right…

BEN *goes into the bedroom.*

Heh. I'm back.

RACHEL. Hi. Is everything alright?

BEN. Fine, yes, fine.

RACHEL. I'm getting my nails done.

BEN. I can see. Do you have to do it in here?

RACHEL. Sorry. We've started now.

BEN. Okay. Well, I'm going to get changed.

MELANIE. He doesn't want to take his clothes off in front of me.

BEN. I have absolutely no qualms in doing that, I was trying, attempting, to be polite.

MELANIE. There's no music to get you started.

A moment. MELANIE *teases* BEN *by singing a song,* BEN *starts to get changed.* SAM *enters the flat.*

SAM. Hello?

MELANIE. We're in here.

SAM *walks through into the bedroom.*

SAM. Hello. Oh. Sorry, Ben, I didn't know you were in a state of undress.

MELANIE. Ignore him.

BEN. It's fine, more the merrier.

SAM. I will give you some space.

BEN. Sam, I'm sure you've seen a lot worse sights in your day job than this.

SAM. Yes, I have.

RACHEL. Good day, Sam?

SAM. Oh yes, very good thanks. I played chess.

BEN. Chess?

SAM. Yes. I'm part of a club.

BEN. Oh right. Great… Are you good?

SAM. I am actually, yes.

BEN. A grandmaster.

SAM. No, that title is only bestowed upon the elite. If you like you could join as well. They're all sorts of levels. Beginners –

BEN. Very kind.

SAM. Every Thursday.

MELANIE. Hear that?

BEN. Yes.

MELANIE. That's an invitation.

RACHEL. You should go.

BEN. I'll keep that in mind.

SAM. I'm just going to put this in our room.

MELANIE. Okay, darling.

SAM *goes to the living room.* BEN *looks over.*

BEN. I'll leave you to it then, shall I, let you get on with –

RACHEL. Thank you.

BEN *heads through to the kitchen.* MELANIE *continues to do* RACHEL*'s nails. They discuss the process.* SAM *joins* BEN *in the kitchen.*

BEN. Fully clothed now.

SAM. If I'd known –

BEN. I will not hear a word that sounds anything like an apology.

SAM. Very well. How was your day?

BEN. It happened. Can I ask you something?

SAM. Yes.

BEN. Don't worry, it's not something weird like what's the oddest thing you've removed from a person's arse.

SAM. A tomato-sauce bottle.

BEN. Oh really, wow, that, there was no hesitation.

SAM. You don't forget it. The man in question slipped. Pure coincidence that it was wrapped in a condom.

BEN. Are we, like, the oddest species in the world? We seem compelled to continually self-destruct.

SAM. Yes.

BEN. Have you always known you wanted to be a doctor?

SAM. Not always, no. Since I was nine.

BEN. You're joking?

SAM. Yes. At secondary school I excelled at sciences. I was told it was irrelevant. That no doctors were ever created at my school.

BEN. That's what you were told?

SAM. Yes, it was made apparent what our horizons were thought to be. I proved them wrong.

BEN. Certainly did. And it turns out you're good at it.

SAM. Yes, very good.

BEN. That's amazing, I love hearing that. Love that belief.

SAM. It's true.

BEN. Exactly, the knowledge. I think there's very little room for being average in this city. Average people are really happy elsewhere. But not here. Not here.

BEN *looks around the flat.*

SAM. What about you, Ben?

BEN. Me? Oh, a communications officer in the civil service. One hundred per cent. Definitely... Remember when you were young, summer holidays, how long they were? Six weeks felt like an eternity. Now six weeks, it's just a beat. I thought time was more friendly than it is.

SAM *smiles, he's not one for indulging. They listen to* MELANIE *and* RACHEL *talking.*

SAM. Would you like to play chess? I have a travel board.

BEN. Erm. Okay. Sure. Yes. Yes. I'll play chess.

SAM *goes through to the living room, sits down.* BEN *follows. As* MELANIE *and* RACHEL *continue to enjoy each other's company.*

Time passes. They politely queue for the bathroom. They sleep. They come in at different times. They bump into each other. They forget to tidy up. They become mildly annoyed at mess that isn't theirs. They spend time in their own rooms. The rooms become less tidy. They fail to notice the flat shrinking.

February

Night-time. Bedroom: RACHEL *is on her bed, writing reports. Living room:* MELANIE *and* SAM *are finishing putting a screen up.*

MELANIE. Are you happy with it there?

SAM. Perhaps a little closer to the wall.

MELANIE. Great thinking, yes, oh perfect, yes. Oh yes, hello privacy. Do you feel better now?

SAM. Is this about yesterday?

MELANIE. You were upset.

SAM. I was extraordinarily tired. The end of four extremely long nights in a row. And the yogurt, to make a fuss about it, it was very petty of me.

MELANIE. No. No. No. It's essential that, if this is to work, you so have to say what's on your mind. Hear that?

SAM. Yes.

MELANIE. Whatever's on your mind.

SAM. Yes. He shouldn't have eaten it.

MELANIE. Too true.

SAM. The thought of that yogurt, it is what got me through the last hour of my shift.

MELANIE. Sam, I'm so in awe of you, you know that? I'm totally aware that this whole idea was mine. I know that they are my friends, well of course they are your friends as well, well you know what I mean –

SAM. Thank you. That's kind. But unnecessary. I came here very much of my own free will.

MELANIE. And I think you're totally amazing for it.

SAM. It was the right solution.

MELANIE. Jesus, I can see my breath. Is the heating not on?

SAM. I would advise you to put another layer on.

MELANIE. Does that mean it's not? Sam, I know you say that hot air rises but we can't rely on the flats below to keep us warm.

SAM. I will go and inspect the boiler.

BEN *enters the flat. He has a bike tyre with him.*

MELANIE. Hi.

BEN. Evening.

BEN *goes straight to the bedroom.*

RACHEL. You're back late.

BEN. I got a fucking puncture.

RACHEL. Oh god, I'm sorry.

BEN. I didn't have a repair kit with me either. Had to push it for a mile and I had all this shopping as well. I need to wash my hands. Put this stuff away for me.

RACHEL. Pardon?

BEN. Can you please put this away.

RACHEL. I'm just in the middle of marking this – of course. Are you leaving that there?

BEN. Where else should I put it?

BEN *goes to the bathroom.* RACHEL *takes the bag through to the kitchen. Starts to unpack.* MELANIE *goes through to the kitchen.*

MELANIE. We've got it up. The screen. Honestly, I can't tell you the difference.

RACHEL. Oh yes, great, makes a massive difference.

BEN *shouts from the bathroom.*

BEN. Rach, can you bring the washing-up liquid?

MELANIE. Dare I ask?

RACHEL. Oil. He got a puncture.

MELANIE. Oh god, I had a puncture once. We were in Amsterdam, riding the bikes, do you remember?

SAM. Melanie…

MELANIE. We were so high.

SAM. We've never been to Amsterdam together.

MELANIE. Oh. No, no we haven't, have we.

SAM. Does Ben need a hand?

RACHEL. Maybe. I don't think he could fix it.

RACHEL *goes through to the kitchen.*

MELANIE. That was pretty bad of me.

SAM. It's fine.

MELANIE. Is it?

RACHEL. Ben, it's empty.

BEN. New bottle. In the bag.

RACHEL. Got it.

RACHEL *goes to the bathroom.* SAM *follows her.*

SAM. I hear you have a puncture.

BEN. Word travels fast.

SAM. Is it a bit fiddly?

BEN. Fiddly?

SAM. Would you like me to have a look at it?

BEN. I'm okay.

SAM. Are you sure? I've repaired a lot.

BEN. I'll be fine. I just need the kit. Thank you. Sam, if you look in my bag in the kitchen there is a yogurt to replace the one I ate.

SAM. You didn't have to do that.

BEN. Well, I did.

SAM. If you find you need any help, do let me know.

SAM *goes up to the kitchen and finds the yogurt. He stays in the kitchen and eats it. Reads the paper.*

BEN. Like I need his help.

RACHEL. He was just being kind.

BEN. He's so passive-aggressive. Getting Mel to send me messages.

RACHEL. What?

BEN. Yeah, Mel sent me a message saying that I should replace his yogurt.

RACHEL. She wouldn't do that.

BEN. Read it if you don't believe me. At least with Jason he would have told me to go and fucking replace it, not get Mel to send me a message.

RACHEL. Don't mention Jay right now. Mel just put her foot in it massively. Saying that she went on holiday to Amsterdam with Sam when it was actually Jay.

BEN. What did he say?

RACHEL. He said it was fine.

BEN. Jesus. Imagine what Jay would have done in that situation.

RACHEL. Thankfully it wasn't, it was somebody who is actually good for her, remember.

BEN. Yeah. I know.

RACHEL. So be nice to him.

BEN. I am.

RACHEL. There's always room for nicer.

MELANIE *goes into the kitchen.*

MELANIE. Hi… oh, that is good to see.

SAM. Did you mention this to Ben?

MELANIE. If I did, it paid off.

SAM. I can voice my own troubles.

MELANIE. Sam?

SAM. What can I do? Melanie?

MELANIE. Voice your own troubles.

A moment. MELANIE *heads back to the living room.*

BEN. The water's just running cold.

RACHEL. Is it the boiler again? Is that why it's so cold in here?

BEN. Fucking hell, I don't know, I'm not a plumber, Rach. Sorry. Sorry.

RACHEL. A chapter.

BEN. Yeah, it's just a chapter.

A brief tender kiss. RACHEL *goes back to the kitchen.*

MELANIE. I'm going in the shower. Did you check the boiler?

SAM. Ben was in the bathroom.

She spots the toothpaste and toilet paper.

MELANIE. You're a lifesaver, I knew there was something I was meant to get.

RACHEL. It was Ben.

MELANIE. I'll take them through, shall I.

She takes them with her.

Thanks for this, Ben.

BEN. What?

MELANIE. For getting these, I saw we'd virtually run out this morning.

BEN. And now we're not.

MELANIE. Totally.

BEN. Four pounds thirty all of that combined.

MELANIE. I tell you what you need to discover: Poundland, it's amazing, everything's a pound.

BEN. I know what fucking Poundland is, Mel.

SAM. Everything alright here?

RACHEL. Ben?

BEN. Yes, fine, thanks.

MELANIE. Your voice is really telling me a different story.

BEN. How perceptive of you.

MELANIE. I'm not a mind-reader, I don't know what's going on in your head.

RACHEL. Ben?

MELANIE. Say what's obviously getting on your nerves.

BEN. Okay. Sure. Okay. I will. Well, there seems to have, a habit has formed, in which I feel like I'm always buying things for the house. Things we all use. I don't know when anyone other than Rachel or I bought toilet paper. Or toothpaste. Or washing-up liquid.

MELANIE. I bought milk yesterday.

BEN. Mel –

MELANIE. Okay, yes, there may well be a point there.

BEN. We've been here four months. It adds up.

MELANIE. Just say that then.

BEN. It's common sense. Do you think it just appears? It's toilet roll, you shove it up your arse, it's not magic.

RACHEL. Alright, Ben, let's just keep it down a level.

SAM. Ben, you're right.

BEN. Thank you.

SAM. Don't let this build up. Articulate. Inform us.

MELANIE. Sam's right, burying what you're thinking is not the way forward here.

BEN. Yes, yes, okay.

MELANIE. We all need to recognise that.

SAM. Openness. That's key. And I think as a group we can do that.

MELANIE. Hear that?

BEN. Yes.

MELANIE. Openness. Two pounds fifteen.

BEN. No.

MELANIE. That's what half is though.

BEN. Don't just give me the money.

MELANIE. You just said it adds up.

BEN. Of course it adds up, they're not free. It's. Don't give me the money. Next time. In future. Just pre-empt it and get stuff.

MELANIE. Okay.

SAM. Yes.

MELANIE. Are we all good here? Great. I'm going in the shower.

She goes into the bathroom. BEN goes back to the bedroom, RACHEL follows. SAM goes to the kitchen and reads a news article.

BEN. It needed to be said. It did. I could have done with your support there, Rach, you know what I was saying was true.

RACHEL. I was right there.

BEN. You didn't say anything to Mel. And now I'm the one that feels like a tosser.

RACHEL. Ben.

BEN. I need you on my side.

RACHEL. There are no sides here.

BEN. You know what I mean. Look, it's fine. It's fine, I've moved on.

RACHEL. Have you?

BEN. I'm fine.

RACHEL. Can I get you a drink?

BEN *nods*. RACHEL *goes to the kitchen*. SAM *is looking at his phone*.

SAM. Extremely depressing.

RACHEL. What's that, Sam?

SAM. According to this article house prices continue to rise –

RACHEL. Oh please don't say that.

SAM. We will have to save even more.

RACHEL. That would be lovely if it was possible.

SAM. It's always possible.

RACHEL. Sam, stop talking.

MELANIE *comes out of the bathroom*.

MELANIE. Er, there's no hot water.

SAM. Let it run.

MELANIE. I have, it's ice-cold.

BEN *comes out of his room*.

BEN. Boiler's on the blink.

MELANIE. What can we do to fix this?

BEN. How are you at plumbing?

SAM. Shall I have a look?

BEN. They teach you a lot at medical school, don't they?

SAM. The light's gone out. I'm going to turn it off and then on again.

BEN. If it works for a computer.

SAM. It needs to stay off for a few seconds.

MELANIE. Has that worked?

RACHEL. Sam?

SAM. No. It won't turn back on.

MELANIE. What does that mean?

BEN. Your hot shower is a no-go.

MELANIE. No. It can't be. We need hot water. We will have to call someone. The estate agents will have an emergency call-out number.

BEN. We can't.

MELANIE. Why not?

RACHEL. We can't really cause a fuss. We've got a good deal here, relatively. The landlord only needs the slightest excuse to get rid of us.

MELANIE. We're not going to be evicted because we complained that the boiler is broken.

RACHEL. Sorry, but I think you're being naive, Mel.

BEN. Regardless of that we couldn't call them out because they'll come round, won't they. And you're here. Both of you. I'll call, but it will have to be in the morning when you're out.

MELANIE. Just say we're guests.

BEN. I think looking round the flat, it's pretty obvious you're not.

RACHEL. It's only twelve hours. Sorry, but it's true.

MELANIE. Hear this?

SAM. Yes.

MELANIE. No hot water. No heating.

SAM. Yes.

MELANIE. Twelve hours!

SAM. You'll be okay till tomorrow.

MELANIE. Oh, will I?

SAM. You know you will.

RACHEL. Just put another layer on.

MELANIE. I shouldn't have to put extra layers on under my own roof!

BEN. Do some star-jumps or some squats then.

MELANIE. This isn't funny.

BEN. No, it's just the way it is.

MELANIE *slams the bathroom door.*

Time passes. They go to their rooms. They moan. They listen to hear what the others are saying. They bump into each other. They stay in their own rooms. They make a drink just for themselves. They discover that things they wanted have run out. They hide things for themselves. The flat becomes smaller.

March

RACHEL *and* BEN *leave the flat.* MELANIE *puts her clothes out to dry in* RACHEL *and* BEN*'s room. Bedroom: clothes are drying on a clothes horse. Living room:* SAM *is doing a puzzle.* MELANIE *is attempting to sleep in the bed. She groans.*

MELANIE. You promised me it would end! I want ibuprofen.

SAM. No. You know the dosage. Two, every four hours.

MELANIE. When's four hours up?

SAM. In three and a half hours.

MELANIE. I'm not drinking ever again. I don't want to do anything today. Curl up. Watch a movie. Can we do that? Whilst we've got the place to ourselves.

SAM. I'd like to complete my puzzle.

MELANIE. You can do your puzzle as well.

SAM. Drink the orange juice, eat the banana. The fructose and potassium will help break down the acetaldehyde. Then I will put a film on.

   MELANIE *smiles.* SAM *sits and starts to do the puzzle.* MELANIE *eats the banana.*

MELANIE. Oh, can you hear that?

SAM. Yes.

MELANIE. Silence.

SAM. Yes.

MELANIE. Just the two of us. This is the future.

   A mobile phone rings. MELANIE *tracks it down. Looks at the number.*

Rachel's ears must be burning. I'm allowed to ignore it, aren't I? It's not bad of me?

MELANIE *puts the phone down.*

We should run around naked.

SAM. Why?

MELANIE. Because we can.

> SAM *smiles, continues with the puzzle.*

> Do you ever think about what we would do if we had this place?

SAM. No.

MELANIE. I just mean, a little daydream that's all. Do you not think about painting, pictures, furniture, the things we'll do, nesting, when we get our own place?

SAM. Yes.

MELANIE. And that excites you?

SAM. Yes. But not here. There are too many problems with this place. Boiler. Mould.

MELANIE. Oh, don't talk about the mould.

SAM. It's growing. /

MELANIE. I don't want to talk about the mould, Sam!

SAM. / This incessant rain is helping it to germinate.

MELANIE. Anyway, at this rate, forget about here and the mould, thinking about owning anywhere can only lead to disappointment.

SAM. No, we will make it happen. Perhaps our sights may not be quite as high as they originally were.

MELANIE. Higher than Ben and Rach's though?

SAM. It's a sliding scale. They will have to reassess as well. Downgrade or go further out.

MELANIE. I'm distracting you from your puzzle.

> SAM *gets back on with his puzzle.* MELANIE *eats, allows herself a little daydream. Footsteps. Both* SAM *and* MELANIE *look up.*

SAM. You told me they were back tomorrow.

MELANIE. Well, that's what they told me.

MELANIE *looks at her phone.*

Oh.

MELANIE *slams herself down on to the bed. The flat door opens.* BEN *and* RACHEL *enter.*

RACHEL.…Is anybody home?

SAM. Yes.

RACHEL. Hi.

MELANIE. Hiya! We weren't expecting you back so soon.

RACHEL. Sorry. We weren't expecting Stevenage to be as hellish as it was. It's so good to be back.

MELANIE. Oh, it's so good to have you back.

BEN. You're a terrible liar.

MELANIE. No, we're really pleased to see you. Aren't we, Sam.

SAM. Yes.

RACHEL. Sam's even worse.

BEN. We don't blame you. I'd be furious if you came back a day early.

RACHEL. I tried calling you. We just couldn't stay, could we?

BEN. No. Not being rude but I need to get out of this mood, I'm going to have a lie-down.

BEN *goes to the bedroom. During the following he takes in the clothes horse. Tries to control his anger. Takes deep breaths.*

RACHEL. He had a massive argument with his brother.

MELANIE. Did he?

RACHEL. Stormed off, I had to pack our bags.

MELANIE. That bad?

RACHEL. Worse.

MELANIE. Can't be as bad as my hangover.

RACHEL. You went out last night?

SAM. She has spent most of the morning with her head down
the toilet.

MELANIE. I was quite violently sick in the toilet.

SAM. Don't worry, I cleaned it.

RACHEL. I thought you two were just staying in.

SAM. So did I.

MELANIE. Don't say it like that. I had no choice, it was
a work do.

RACHEL. Oh god, I'd love a night out. What are they like?

MELANIE. Had such a blast. Went up The Shard. Fifty-second
floor! Seriously, you'd love it. Cocktails to die for. The most
amazing panoramic city view. I gave the flat a shout-out.

RACHEL. You went up The Shard?

MELANIE. Yep, look out of the window and last night that was
me. God, I needed to let my hair down. Can't expect me to
just sit at home and do puzzles all night with him.

SAM. Preferably.

MELANIE. What is the point of living in London if you don't
get to experience its delights, eh?

BEN. Rach?!

RACHEL. Yeah?!

MELANIE. Oh, easy on the volume.

RACHEL. Sorry.

BEN. Can you come here.

> RACHEL *heads to the bedroom.* MELANIE *mouths 'Fuck's
> sake'.* SAM *nods. Carries on with his puzzle. In the bedroom.*

I'm speechless.

RACHEL. Okay. So they weren't expecting us back.

BEN. This is not the time to prove your good nature.

RACHEL. It's just some clothes.

BEN. It's a liberty.

RACHEL. Quiet.

BEN. It's an absolute liberty. And I want them out.

RACHEL. Okay. Okay. Yes.

> RACHEL *and* BEN *head back to the living room.*

> Hi. You really weren't expecting us back, were you?
> Slightly awkward. Sorry, but you've left a clothes horse in
> our bedroom.

BEN. On our bed.

RACHEL. Ben –

BEN. With all your clothes still on.

MELANIE. Oh god, it's got all my underwear on, hasn't it.

BEN. I don't really have an encyclopaedic knowledge of all
your underwear, but there were certainly lots of different
colours, shapes, fabrics and –

MELANIE. . Are they dry?

BEN. Funnily enough, I didn't touch any of the things.

MELANIE. I don't mind.

BEN. I'm not going to go and touch your pants, Mel.

MELANIE. Don't say pants – I'm not a toddler.

BEN. Your knickers.

MELANIE. Underwear.

BEN. Underwear. I'm not going to go back and touch them.

MELANIE. You want me to move them?

RACHEL. Please.

BEN. Just go and move them, Mel.

MELANIE. Is this because you've had an argument with your brother?

BEN. No, it's because you're using our room like a Chinese laundry.

MELANIE. We weren't expecting you back.

BEN. That's clearly not the point here.

MELANIE. Fine. Sam?

SAM. I'm in the midst of my puzzle.

MELANIE. It's not going anywhere.

SAM. No, Melanie. You'll have to do it yourself.

MELANIE *gets up. She goes to the bedroom.*

RACHEL. How's the puzzle going?

SAM. Frustrating. One piece is proving terribly elusive.

RACHEL. Do you want a hand?

SAM. No.

BEN. Perhaps it's not in the box.

SAM. Of course it is.

MELANIE *exits the bedroom with the clothes horse. She puts it up in the corridor.*

BEN. Seriously, Mel.

MELANIE. What? I'm not allowed it in the corridor, am I?

BEN. What do you want me to say, that you can just put them where you want? Well, I'm not going to. I'm not going to spend my evening climbing over your clothes just to move around this flat.

MELANIE. Do you hear me complain about your bike crap?

BEN. That's always temporary, whilst I repair it.

MELANIE. And what's this if it's not temporary??!! Even in this frozen wasteland things still dry.

BEN. It's a million miles from being the same thing.

MELANIE. Where do you want me to put it?

BEN. In your room. Like we do.

MELANIE. Sam's in the middle of his puzzle.

BEN. Why is that my problem?

MELANIE. Rach, have a word.

RACHEL. Ben, shall we just go to our room.

BEN. Are you taking their side? You normally moan to me about the washing being out.

RACHEL. Okay, that's enough.

MELANIE. Is this true, Rach?

RACHEL. It's been a taxing day.

BEN. Too right it has and this is just making it worse.

MELANIE. Move your puzzle, Sam.

SAM. Wait.

RACHEL. Mel, there's no need to disrupt Sam's puzzle.

MELANIE. Clearly there is.

RACHEL *grabs the clothes horse, her and* MELANIE *tussle over it.*

It's not my fault you've come back early.

BEN. Typical, making it someone else's fault. She's as bad as Stevenage.

MELANIE. Did you just call me Stevenage?

BEN. So what if I did?

MELANIE. What does that even mean?

BEN. Stevenage. Stevenage! STEVENAGE!

MELANIE. Why are you acting like such a wanker?

BEN. This is not being a wanker, this is about expressing a
massive amount of resentment about how you've intruded,
broken our privacy with a –

SAM. A clothes horse.

BEN. Yes, yes with a clothes horse. And yes, a clothes horse
probably shouldn't get on my nerves but it does. I mean, it
really does. And I may feel like a tosser in the morning for
saying so, but right now I don't feel at all like one. Or maybe
I do. Yeah, yeah, I do. I'm a tosser. A massive one. Fucking
clothes horse. Jesus, Ben. Sorry. Sorry. Mel. Sorry, everyone.
Mel, it's fine in the corridor. Just ignore what I said about it.
It's. God. Ahhh. I've just, well, I've found the last few days
rather depressing. Stevenage. Bloody Stevenage. Well, it's
not Stevenage per say. Places like that, Aldershot, Crawley,
you know those places you normally go by on a high-speed
train and don't understand why anyone would want to get off
there? Oh god, the look of them. Flat. Spawning identikit
houses for miles. Culturally bereft. Geographically insipid.
I'm not one to get all biblical, but they're always the first
places to get flooded and they barely have rivers running
through them; it's like, come on, take the hint, even God
hates you! The only reason for these places is because people
can't go any further from London. So everyone spends their
life on trains or in the car. And the people who live there
become zombies. That's what my brother has become. And
my brother, I can't say it really in any other way, is, was kind
of my hero. He played drums in a band and, and years ago
when I was sixteen, I visited him when he first moved here
and he took me out and sneaked me into clubs and I got
really pissed and he had tattoos before every single person in
the world had them and he dated some really beautiful
women. And this sounds really crap, I know, but I held him
up on such a pedestal and now, now he desperately wants to
but can't afford a house with space for his two kids
anywhere close to what we'd call London. So he moved out
to Stevenage and he lives in a house that looks like a piece of

Lego. And he just looks so sad. And he knows he does. And he can't do anything to change that. So he's become cruel and decided to take it out on me by saying that the same thing will happen to me, as if it can happen to him, someone who is a thousand times more successful than I am, then I, we, will share the same fate. And the truth is beyond all that cruelty he is a hundred per cent right. One hundred per cent.

SAM. Are you finished?

RACHEL. He is.

SAM. Self-pity is a horribly ugly trait, Ben.

BEN. What did you just say?

SAM. Talking in such a manner. Moping. It won't help you achieve what you want, will it.

BEN. Have you listened to anything I just said?!

SAM. Unfortunately, yes.

SAM*'s phone rings. He looks at the name. Answers it.*

Yes, Mum.

MELANIE. Sam.

SAM. It's my mum.

MELANIE. Go into the kitchen.

SAM. Wait. I have to go into the kitchen.

SAM *exits. He continues on the call. His conversation is as follows:*

(Hi. Are you okay? He has. Oh. Are you okay? Should I come home? Sure. Of course. Let me know if you change your mind. Okay. Love you too. Bye, Mum. Bye.)

SAM *sits by himself, takes in the news. Listens to the conversation. Meanwhile…*

MELANIE. Look, he's not very subtle but I think Sam is right.

RACHEL. Oh my god, Mel.

MELANIE. It's easy to be negative.

BEN. I'm not being negative. I'm being honest. I'm just being fucking realistic, that's what. Those two choices: live like this or that.

RACHEL. This is just raw. It all feels raw.

BEN. It can't be that. It can't be. I was told go to university. Do well and you will be rewarded. And I've done that. You've done that. It's not asking for much.

MELANIE. Ben, there are other cities, it's not all Stevenage or London.

BEN. Of course there are other cities, but be realistic, Mel, this is where all roads lead to. It's where all the money's pumped in to. We're trapped.

MELANIE. No, no you're not. Teachers can go anywhere.

BEN. I'm not a teacher.

MELANIE. Rachel is. See, it's not all doom and gloom. And, Ben, you don't even like your job, your job, be honest, you could get a job like that elsewhere.

BEN. For fuck's sake, Mel, that's not the point.

MELANIE. I'm just trying to put a silver lining out there.

RACHEL. Sorry, sorry, but I don't understand why it's okay to say that though. 'You're a teacher you could get a job elsewhere.' Yes. Yes, maybe it's true. But if we all went with that concept who is going to teach those who live here? Who is going to do that, Mel?

MELANIE. I'm not arguing with you.

RACHEL. The fact that you even said that though. It actually came out of your mouth. Have you not heard me telling you about some of the kids that I teach? We think we have problems, man alive. Makes me feel so angry with myself for moaning about our predicament, but I think, I think I really do deserve the chance to do so. I don't want to not

be a teacher. I don't want to leave the kids to be taught by,
I don't know, I actually don't know who in the future will
end up teaching them.

BEN. That's all part of the master plan, though, as soon, they'll
have finished shipping them off to Stoke, or other places
where they don't blight the city, and the only job a teacher
could have is at somewhere like Dulwich Prep.

MELANIE. I've not phrased this well.

RACHEL. No, no you haven't. This city is our home. Fifteen
years. We've been here since the same date.

MELANIE. Yes.

RACHEL. Ben even longer. Why should we have to go?

MELANIE. You shouldn't.

RACHEL. I love this city. I adore it. It's home. I love the noise.
The scale of it. The fact that every corner has history. Try
finding history on every corner of Stevenage, you fucking
can't, it's just Greggs or charity shops.

BEN. Don't forget you can actually use public transport as a
positive lifestyle choice. /

RACHEL. Here, we live in a city that embraces difference.

BEN. / The Tube, I mean come on, the bloody Tube!

RACHEL. There's a tolerance and openness that just doesn't
exist elsewhere. /

BEN. Every nationality. Religion. Race. Orientation.

RACHEL. / The whole world exists within four square miles.
That's before I even start talking about the restaurants,
galleries, theatres, bars –

BEN. The Shard.

RACHEL. Yes, The Shard, I should be able to go up The Shard!

MELANIE. Yes, yes you should.

RACHEL. But I can't! I can't.

SAM. Of course you can, there's not even a booking process.

BEN. That's grown up, shouting things from another room.

SAM *walks back into the room.*

SAM. The bar is open to all on a first-come, first-served basis. The policy is on their website.

RACHEL. Very funny being so very facetious.

BEN. You really don't fucking understand, Sam.

SAM. You're doing it again, Ben. Pity. Where does this pity come from, it comes from a position of entitlement.

BEN. Entitlement, are you mad? Look at us.

SAM. Your mindset. You went to university. Yes. So have many millions of others. What makes you different to them? They have all been told the same story. Yet you expect something unique for yourself.

BEN. Rach, let's go to our room before I say something I won't be able to take back.

RACHEL. Not going to be preached at by those two moneybags.

MELANIE. Those two, what? Hear that, Sam?

SAM. Yes.

MELANIE. Moneybags?!

SAM. Yes.

RACHEL. Easy to be flippant about this, to provoke, because in the long run, you earn decent money.

MELANIE. Hardly decent.

RACHEL. Way to rub it in! You earn way more than me. And Sam, he's a doctor. His wages are almost double mine and Ben's, between you, you'll earn enough for you to live comfortably here.

SAM. Yes. That is true. And there is your solution.

BEN. Why now do you keep talking?

SAM. Somebody has to say this to you. Earn more money if that is what you desire. Work harder for it or choose a new line of work.

RACHEL. You think what I get paid as a teacher is okay, do you?

SAM. That is irrelevant. When you started your job you knew what you'd get paid. Do not blame us. Do not blame the restrictions that were already in place with your job. You can blame lack of ambition.

BEN. Fuck off.

SAM. No. You cannot always have your hand held. You have made a choice to want to live here, to do the job you do. Respect that choice or change. Or do you still believe the adage that London is a city where the streets are paved with gold? Well, it isn't. People have had to move out and commute from towns such as Stevenage for years, the search and desire for space is nothing new or sad, it is a fact.

MELANIE. Sam –

SAM. No, Melanie, let me finish. This is an expensive city. It does not attempt to hide it. There is a very clear reason why people are being rehoused to other towns and cities, it is because they provide better value for money for the taxpayer.

RACHEL. They're not numbers, they're people, with lives and families and history –

SAM. A history that very few would wish to have.

BEN. Easy for you to say –

SAM. It is, yes. As it is my history. I have lived it. Not read about it on the *Guardian* website. I worked hard to escape it. Some I lived alongside didn't. Now I have a future. They don't. And I will have no nostalgia for that as a way of life from people who have never lived it. Yes, Ben? I have no qualms continuing this conversation. It is an area I am extremely well versed in.

BEN *knows he is likely to lose.*

BEN. Such a tosser.

BEN *storms off out of the flat.*

RACHEL. Ben, wait!

MELANIE. Wait. Don't go as well.

RACHEL. What, and let him storm off!

MELANIE. I don't want to be doing this. It's horrible.

RACHEL. If that comes out of your mouth imagine what comes out of those that don't actually have any interest in us.

MELANIE. I don't ever want money or jobs to be what defines us, yeah. Fifteen years, yeah, that's what does. Hear that?

RACHEL. Not at the moment.

RACHEL *goes off after* BEN.

MELANIE. What the hell has got in to you?

SAM. All I hear from them is how hard the world is for them. Well, it isn't.

MELANIE. You can't say that to them even if you think it.

SAM. Who else will then?

MELANIE. You could see he was vulnerable.

SAM. That is not vulnerable, Melanie!

SAM *goes to his puzzle.*

MELANIE. Don't just go over there and play your puzzle.

SAM. You don't play a puzzle!

MELANIE. Sam?

SAM. –

MELANIE. Sam?

SAM. –

MELANIE. Sam?

SAM. What?

MELANIE. Talk to me. You promised me you wouldn't just shut down like this. I can't guess what's going on in there.

SAM. My uncle has died. That's why my mum phoned.

MELANIE. What?

SAM. My uncle has died. That's why my mother phoned.

MELANIE. Oh god, Sam, I'm so sorry. Are you okay?

SAM. Yes.

MELANIE. Are you? Sam, I didn't even know you had an uncle.

SAM. I did.

SAM *goes back to his puzzle. Stops.*

He moved to Canada when I was very young. He wanted a better life. He wanted me and my mum to come with him. We didn't. He got hit by a drunk driver. If it helps avoid future tension, I will apologise when they return.

SAM *continues with his puzzle.*

Time passes. They nod hello. They sleep. They grow restless. They don't do the washing up. They don't take the bins out. They go to their rooms. They avoid each other. They become aware that the flat is smaller. MELANIE *spends less time in the flat.* SAM *is left by himself.*

April

SAM *is waiting up for* MELANIE *in the living room. He is drawn to listening to what is happening next door.* BEN *and* RACHEL *are in bed, an attempt at intimacy.* RACHEL *starts and then continues to cough throughout.*

BEN. Rach?

RACHEL. Don't stop.

BEN. What you doing?

RACHEL. I'm getting close.

BEN. You're coughing.

RACHEL. Don't worry, just keep doing that.

He carries on. She continues to cough.

BEN. Are you sure you're alright?

RACHEL. Very, very sure. Down. /

BEN. I'm trying /

RACHEL. Little bit more. /

BEN. it's hard to keep /

RACHEL. There.

BEN. / in the same place with you coughing.

RACHEL. Shhh…

BEN. This is weird. Seriously.

RACHEL. Shhhh…

BEN. This is not working for me.

RACHEL. Ben, don't –

BEN. It's killed it. Why are you fucking coughing?

RACHEL. Sam can hear otherwise.

BEN. That's mental. Coughing! Put some music on.

RACHEL. That's just even more obvious.

BEN. Fuck's sake. It's been weeks.

RACHEL. Longer. What do you want me to say? He's right there. There. I can almost touch him.

BEN. Jesus, we can't even touch each other any more.

RACHEL....

BEN. I'm going for a piss.

> BEN *gets up and goes to the bathroom.* RACHEL *stays in bed, dejected.* MELANIE *returns. She's slightly drunk.*

MELANIE. I'm late I know.

SAM. Again.

MELANIE. I was working.

SAM. In a bottle of wine?

MELANIE. It's called networking.

SAM. I've been waiting up for you.

MELANIE. Never asked you to.

SAM. I really need to talk to you.

MELANIE. And I really need water.

SAM. It can wait. Please, sit down.

> MELANIE *ignores* SAM *and goes through to the kitchen.* BEN *exits from the bathroom. He goes straight back into the bedroom. Sits on the edge of the bed.*

RACHEL. Shall we go away? A couple of nights. A little hotel by the sea.

BEN. We can't, we've got to save. We're nearly halfway there.

RACHEL. I know.

BEN. Even a couple of nights in the cheapest of places would derail our target.

RACHEL. For our own sanity.

BEN. We can't afford it.

RACHEL. Well, a night out.

BEN. Where? Nowhere's free? Can hardly go and sit in the park in this weather, can we?

RACHEL. We're not even making use of the city.

BEN. Think I don't know?! I know, Rach.

RACHEL. Hannah and Sean invited us round for dinner, that's a night out, the cost of a bottle of wine.

BEN. And spend a night being quizzed on this?

RACHEL. They wouldn't do that.

BEN. Of course that's what they'd do. That's all anyone ever asks.

RACHEL. So now even our other friends are off-limits, are they?

BEN *lies on the bed with* RACHEL. *They stare at the ceiling.* MELANIE *goes back to the living room with her glass of water.*

SAM. Sit down.

MELANIE. Stop telling me to sit down.

SAM. Melanie, you're being too loud.

MELANIE. I want to be able to talk normally.

SAM. Well, you can't. So as I asked, please sit down and listen.

MELANIE. Fine.

SAM. I was hoping to talk to you about this when you were sober.

MELANIE. Well, I'm not. Just say what you want to say.

SAM. My mum called earlier. She had news about her brother. There was a reading of his will. He left my mum some money. What turns out to be a substantial amount of money. And my mum wants to donate a lot of that money to me.

MELANIE. What are you telling me?

SAM. Sixty thousand pounds.

MELANIE. Sixty?

SAM. Yes.

MELANIE. Sixty?

SAM. Yes.

MELANIE. Not six?

SAM. No.

MELANIE. Can we take that from her?

SAM. She was insistent. She would not know how to spend it on herself.

MELANIE *starts to cry.*

MELANIE. Does that mean it can actually happen?

SAM. Yes.

MELANIE. Really?

SAM. Yes. I spoke to a mortgage adviser. There would be no problem now.

MELANIE. Oh god, you're telling me that our dreams can actually come true, and I'm just a drunken mess, who doesn't even answer your calls, who just leaves you here by yourself. I'm so sorry, Sam, do you hear?

SAM. Yes.

MELANIE. So sorry.

SAM. Yes.

MELANIE. I just needed a night out from here.

SAM. It's okay.

MELANIE. Snot and tears, they are all one. Oh god, Sam, what about… Have you told them?

SAM. I was waiting to tell you first.

MELANIE. Good.

SAM. Shall we go and tell them now?

MELANIE. Yes!

SAM. Okay.

MELANIE. Wait, no! God, no. What would I say? That we've just inherited sixty thousand pounds? That we have more than enough money for a deposit?

SAM. That is what has happened.

MELANIE. I don't think this is the sort of news we can share. They'll be, won't they be jealous and angry, will they be that?

SAM. We'd be happy for them, wouldn't we?

MELANIE. Would we? Yes we would. Of course we would.

MELANIE *hugs* SAM. *They kiss. Passionate. Months of frustration being released.* BEN *and* RACHEL *have been lying in their bed, trying to sleep, but failing.* RACHEL *gets up and goes to the kitchen.* BEN *ignores her exiting.*

RACHEL.…Mel…?

MELANIE *and* SAM *stop.*

MELANIE. Rach?

RACHEL. Sorry… I'm sorry… Mel…

MELANIE. Are you okay?

RACHEL. Would you, could you come here?

MELANIE. In there?

RACHEL. Please. Yes. You're not asleep, are you?

MELANIE. No, no, totally not asleep.

RACHEL. Sorry.

MELANIE. I'm coming.

RACHEL. Thank you.

MELANIE *mouths 'Sorry' to* SAM *and then goes to the kitchen.*

MELANIE. Hi.

RACHEL. Have you been out?

MELANIE. Work thing, yeah. I didn't wake you, did I?

RACHEL. I wasn't asleep.

MELANIE.…Rach?

RACHEL. You look happy.

MELANIE. That's two bottles of wine for you. Are you okay?

RACHEL *shakes her head. She can barely speak. She points towards her room.*

RACHEL. All we talk about is money… that's all we do. Sit in there and. That or silence. I…

MELANIE *goes and hugs* RACHEL. *They stay there.* BEN *continues to stare at the ceiling.*

SAM *waits for* MELANIE *to return.*

Time passes. The flat gets smaller. They squeeze past each other. They tread on each other's toes. They fail to sleep. They ignore each other.

May

BEN *is in the bathroom.* MELANIE *waits outside.* RACHEL *hovers.*

MELANIE. Tell him to hurry up –

RACHEL. It is actually his /

MELANIE. Ben!

RACHEL. / allotted time.

MELANIE. I'm going to be late.

RACHEL. Mel, there's no other way to say it: you missed your slot.

MELANIE. I overslept – stone me.

RACHEL. Well, that's not Ben's fault, is it? Mel?

MELANIE. Wow, you've changed your tune, thought everything was his fault.

RACHEL. Mel!

  RACHEL *exits to the kitchen in disgust.* BEN *sticks his head out of the bathroom.*

BEN. Stop banging on the door.

MELANIE. Oh, you're finally done?

BEN. No, I've just gone in.

MELANIE. I'm going to be late.

BEN. Don't have a shower then.

MELANIE. Are you for real?

BEN. What, so I'll get out, let you do what you've got to do, and I'll be late instead?

MELANIE. As if it matters what time you get in.

BEN. It was you that created these windows of time. If you want a shower, you're going to have to wait. Be late. It's happened to me enough when you've overrun. I have fifteen minutes more and I am going to use every single one of them.

BEN *closes the door to the bathroom.* MELANIE *goes to the kitchen.*

RACHEL. Sorry, that was really uncalled for, really unnecessary, to imply that I was unhappy with Ben.

MELANIE. It's not me that said Ben should be earning more.

RACHEL. I. Did not. If I said that it was –

MELANIE. You did.

RACHEL. It was a slip of the tongue. A mistake. Made in private. To you. Only you. I trust you still know what that word means.

RACHEL *exits the kitchen. She bumps into* SAM *who enters the flat.*

SAM. Morning.

RACHEL. Yes. There's some coffee made, if you want some.

SAM. No, I've just worked a night shift, I want to sleep.

RACHEL *goes to her bedroom. Sits on the bed. Counts to twenty.*

You're not dressed.

MELANIE. I'm waiting for the shower.

SAM. It's not your time slot. You're going to be late.

MELANIE. What on earth is helpful about saying that?

SAM *takes* MELANIE*'s arm and escorts her into the living room.*

SAM. I would like you to stop talking to me in that tone.

MELANIE. It's Ben fault, he's really pushing me –

SAM. Stop there. Excuses show you're not in what? Melanie?

MELANIE. Control.

SAM. Exactly. I need you to be in control.

MELANIE. He's doing it deliberately though…

SAM. Then you must rise above it. Now listen closely. Melanie, the flat we looked at, the one that we both loved, that we were told was off the market, well, the sale has fallen through. The estate agent has left me a message informing me, asking, if we want to make an offer. I believe we need to do this.

MELANIE. Sam.

SAM. We should make an offer today. ASAP.

MELANIE. We can't, we can't do it to them. We have another six months here.

SAM. Do we?

MELANIE. We made an agreement. As hellish as it can be, yeah, we can't do that, they would hate us.

SAM. A sale doesn't go through overnight. It could take months. Our own place, Melanie. I do not want to waste time. If we don't act now then later we may not be able to. The prices every day –

BEN *shouts from the bathroom.*

BEN. You owe me. Quicker than a prison shower that.

MELANIE. It's not funny, I'm totally late. You hear?

BEN. No.

MELANIE. Late!

BEN. You're going to be late?!

MELANIE. I'm not laughing!

BEN *approaches in a towel. He hovers at the door.*

BEN. Look, nobody here is laughing. Quite clearly no one here is going, 'This is brilliant.' This is not what any of us imagined when they said, 'Grow up, move out, get a job, have your own space.' It's not the dream, okay. No one would sell this dream. It's shit. But it is what it is –

MELANIE. Can you just shut up, Ben. Seriously, yeah, always thirty words when one would do. And put some clothes on, no one's impressed with that.

BEN *goes to his room, gets ready.* MELANIE *stares at* SAM.

Rachel and I didn't always share a room in our first year. Rachel had her own room when we began. She was that lucky one in nine. The privacy. The luxury of it. I didn't have that. I shared with this horrible, horrible girl. Sally Crosby. Rachel swapped with Sally. She gave up that luxury so that my experience would be less horrific... Sam...

SAM. I admire your nobility. But this option is the future. You and I are the future, aren't we? Melanie?

MELANIE. Yes.

SAM. To pick up the phone and call and make an offer is the future.

MELANIE. I really want to be able to agree with you. But...

A moment. MELANIE *goes into the bathroom.* SAM *attempts to bury his frustration.*

Oh my god, oh my, that is disgusting, Ben.

BEN. Yeah.

MELANIE. What is wrong with you? Couldn't you have waited till you got to work?

BEN. Perhaps, it would have been a risk, but if I'm being honest, I purposely did the worst dump I could ever possibly do especially for you. Complements the steam. Enjoy.

RACHEL. You better hurry up, Mel, those vitally important leaflets won't choose their font themselves.

A moment. BEN *and* RACHEL *go back into the bedroom.* MELANIE *heads back into the living room.*

SAM. Melanie?

MELANIE. Do it.

SAM. Yes? Are you sure?

MELANIE. Yes. I, we, can't keep doing this. Make an offer.

SAM *nods.* MELANIE *stares at the adjoining wall.*
RACHEL *is saddened by her choice of words.* BEN *puts*
his arm round her. Time passes. The flat gets smaller. And
smaller. And they are aware of it. They suffer rejection.
They circle each other. Two packs. Wary. Waiting to strike.

June

MELANIE *and* SAM *are out.* RACHEL *and* BEN *are*
attempting to empty the bin.

BEN. It's dripping.

RACHEL. Get another bag.

BEN. My hands are full.

RACHEL. Careful.

   It splits. Contents pour out and on to the floor.

BEN. Jesus Christ.

RACHEL. Ben!

BEN. Stupid fucking bag!

RACHEL. I said to be careful!

BEN. Do you think I did it on purpose? Fucking hell, Rach!

   BEN *kicks the rubbish around the kitchen.* RACHEL
   watches on.

   It's always me, this. Always me! My entire life is spent
   emptying bins. All their crap!!

   BEN *eventually stops. Stares at the mess. A moment.*

RACHEL. Finished?

   BEN *nods.* RACHEL *offers* BEN *a sweet.*

Yesterday was seven months. The scale has tipped. We've been here longer than we have left. The tunnel, the light, it's there. Make a wish.

A moment. BEN *eats the sweet.*

Now, shall we tidy this up?

BEN *nods. He picks up the contents. Starts putting them into another bag.* BEN *spots something in the bag. He takes it out. Stares at it. Hunts for more. It's a piece of ripped up paper. He tries to match the pieces.*

What are you doing? Ben? Ben?

BEN *holds up the pieces of paper, holds them together.*

BEN. Read this, just read it.

RACHEL *takes the piece of paper.*

FUCKING CUNTS.

RACHEL. I don't understand.

BEN. I think that's pretty self-explanatory. See the name on the top. Dr Sam Grant. They've been bidding on flats. Look, offer rejected. June the fifteenth. Two weeks ago. I knew something was going on, I fucking knew it.

RACHEL. It must be a mistake, Mel wouldn't do that.

BEN. Wouldn't she?

RACHEL. No. She's not said anything to me.

BEN. Fuck's sake, Rach, she doesn't deserve that pedestal you've put her on.

Footsteps in the distance.

RACHEL. That's them. What should I do with this?

BEN. Keep it.

Front door opens. MELANIE *and* SAM *enter.*

MELANIE. Hello.

SAM. What's that smell?

BEN. This.

MELANIE. Oh dear, split bin. Nasty. I hate it when that happens.

BEN. Wouldn't you have to have emptied a bin to know what that's like?

SAM. Melanie.

MELANIE. Sorry, yeah, would love to chat, but flying visit.

BEN. Actually we just wanted a quick word.

MELANIE. Well, like I said, flying visit –

BEN. A few minutes for your 'roomies', you can do that.

SAM. We will be back in a couple of hours.

RACHEL. Have you been bidding on flats?

MELANIE. What?

RACHEL. Have you been bidding on flats?

MELANIE. Why are you asking that?

RACHEL. Why aren't you answering? Have you been bidding on flats? Mel?

MELANIE. Yes. Yes we have. Rach...

SAM. Have you been rummaging in our room?

BEN. No.

SAM. You were rummaging in the bin?

BEN. No, Sam, we're not raccoons, the fucking bin bag split.

MELANIE. We were going to tell you.

RACHEL. But you didn't.

MELANIE. Been so close to. I really wanted to. There's never been the right time. We didn't want you to find out like this.

SAM. No.

MELANIE. It's a relief.

BEN. What?

MELANIE. Yes. We've been desperate to tell you, and other people, but we've not been able to. It's been so hard.

RACHEL. Are you kidding me? You're turning this into your struggle.

BEN. I don't understand, how is it possible for you to bid on a flat?

SAM. Straightforward. You view, you make an offer.

BEN. Are you for real?

SAM. I answered your question.

BEN. Financially!

SAM. I was left money by my uncle.

BEN. Right. I think we deserve more than just that.

MELANIE. What, you want us to be crude and talk about figures and amounts?

BEN. Of course I fucking do!

SAM. Sixty thousand.

BEN. Sixty thousand pounds?

SAM. Yes.

BEN. Jesus fucking Christ.

SAM. It was unexpected.

BEN. Why, because you barely knew the man?

RACHEL. How long have you known about the money?

MELANIE. Six weeks.

RACHEL. You've lied for six weeks?

MELANIE. We haven't lied, we've just not said anything.

RACHEL. You have lied. We talked about the amount of savings we had only last week and you didn't even blink. You lied to me.

MELANIE. How easy do you think that was for me? I was protecting you.

RACHEL. Protecting?

SAM. Melanie has found this extraordinarily hard, Rachel. I told her that we'd be happy for you if the scenario was the other way round. But she told me I was wrong, that nobody understands good fortune.

MELANIE. Sam, stop. This is such an impossible scenario. We want the same for you.

BEN. Oh, how noble.

SAM. Of course we do.

MELANIE. We couldn't not accept the money, could we?

RACHEL. You lied to me. Lied, Mel. How long, how many have you bid on?

MELANIE. You really want to do this?

RACHEL. Yes.

MELANIE. A month. Hundreds of offers. Well, not hundreds but it's not easy out there, you know, it's not all smiles, it's stressful /

BEN. Boohoo.

MELANIE. / brutal, despite all this talk of it slowing down, it took many offers, countless rejections /

SAM. Six.

MELANIE. / before we finally had one accepted.

RACHEL. Accepted?

MELANIE. Yes. We have had an offer accepted.

RACHEL. Accepted? What on? Where? What? Tell me.

MELANIE. A two-bed. Garden flat. No chain. Off Lordship Lane.

RACHEL. How much? Say it. How much?

MELANIE. Really?

RACHEL. Yes, fucking really.

SAM. Five hundred and sixty thousand.

RACHEL. Five hundred and sixty thousand?

SAM. Yes.

BEN. That's not possible. That's nearly double our budget. There's no way even with a ten per cent deposit you would be able to secure that.

SAM. We have. We have a fifteen per cent deposit. The bank will loan us the rest.

BEN. That's four hundred and seventy-odd thousand pounds. Are you mad? That's so much money. When interest rates rise in a few years you'll be screwed. It will be crippling. You'll be out on the street. You'll be fucked.

SAM. No, we won't. We are locked into five years at a very low rate and by then if they do rise, we will be fine. Both Melanie and I work in a profession where we can expect to see a healthy rise in wages over the coming years. The most important act is being on the ladder. Prices will continue to rise. Perhaps less aggressively, but they will rise. We will make money. We will be fine.

BEN. Oh good, good for you.

RACHEL. What's going to happen to us?

MELANIE. Us?

RACHEL. Yes. To this flat. Us.

BEN. There's five months left on the contract.

SAM. We're not leaving tomorrow.

MELANIE. Exactly, you don't just complete overnight. Think about how great this will be. We can go back to how things were.

BEN. Were?

MELANIE. As friends. Not this. On top of each other. In each other's pockets. We're sick of the sight of each other.

BEN. Oh I'm sorry. It's not something we've loved either. This is not meant to be fun. This is meant to be hard. It's meant to be a sacrifice.

MELANIE. And it has been. And we always knew it would come to an end.

RACHEL. So you're going to pay the rest of the contract.

SAM. What?

RACHEL. If you complete before this contract finishes.

SAM. Rachel, if that happens, we wouldn't be able to pay for two places. Especially one we will not live in. It's not a cheap mortgage. Our disposable income will sharply decline.

RACHEL. What, so you'd just fuck off? Leave us high and dry?

SAM. That sounds cold the way you phrased it.

RACHEL. How else could I phrase it? You can't do that to us. We wouldn't be able to save. All our money will go on rent. We'd be set back a year.

SAM. You could rent out the living room.

RACHEL. Who to?

SAM. That would be your decision.

BEN. No, no, you can't move out. Simple as that. You wouldn't leave us in the lurch.

SAM. Ben.

BEN. You'd pay us out.

MELANIE. We can talk about this.

BEN. I want to hear you say it. Say you would pay us out.

RACHEL. Say it, Mel.

MELANIE. I…

BEN. Say it.

SAM. We are not on any contract.

BEN. Yes we are. One of the first things we did was sign that contract.

SAM. That was a bit of scruffy handwritten paper. A bit of fun. That's not legally binding.

RACHEL. I thought it carried more weight than that. You're supposed to be my best friend.

MELANIE. I am. Is it an apology you want? We should have done this slightly better, yes. I accept that. It was an error. But we have to look after our future. And we need every single penny we have. And I can't apologise for that. And if you want me to apologise for being ahead of you in the game, I can't. It's the way it is.

RACHEL. The way it is?!

SAM. Yes, it's not our fault we can afford it and you can't.

BEN. Afford it?! You were given it on a plate!

MELANIE. You know deep down in the long run we would have been able to, ahead of you. I'm sorry, but that's true.

RACHEL. Oh my god what's happened to you? You're a mercenary.

MELANIE. I'm a realist.

RACHEL. You've bought in to it haven't you, this mantra running through the country. The powers-that-be. We're being driven so mad, so blind, we're being turned against each other. It used to just be the poor against the rich but now everyone's at it.

SAM. This is not political.

RACHEL. Oh yes, it fucking is, look at us sniping at each other. Friends. Best friends. We've become savages trampling over each other for a tiny bit of grass. Have we got to spend our life praying that someone we love, or know, dies before we can make owning a home a possibility? Is that what we've got to do? Pray my gran cops it so I can get a one-bed in Nunhead. Fucking hell. I don't want to be that person, I really don't.

MELANIE. We didn't plan this. It's not our fault.

SAM. You would do the same in our situation.

RACHEL. Do you really think that, Melanie? You're not going to answer me? Is this his doing?

MELANIE. No.

RACHEL. I always thought you were just a reliable person. Somebody who cares about Mel.

SAM. That's who I am.

RACHEL. Then what have you turned her in to? For all his flaws, Jason would never have done this, never turned her into a fucking Tory.

MELANIE. I'm not a Tory.

SAM. Jason, he wouldn't have even been able to get a mortgage on a cardboard box.

BEN. At least he wasn't a boring cunt. Yeah, I can say that now. You're a boring cunt!

SAM. That language impresses no one.

BEN. I've got plenty more where that came from. Fucking chess club!

SAM. That is not an insult!

RACHEL. You can't shit straight.

MELANIE. What?

RACHEL. Every time he goes for a shit it's always left on the side of the bowl.

SAM. That is not true.

RACHEL. I'm not one of your nurses, I'm not going to clean up your shit. Just sit in the middle of the bowl. Or have you got a wonky anus?!

MELANIE. Leave him alone.

BEN. Oh are you feeling left out because it's not about you? The ego on you! /

RACHEL. Get a colleague to check it out.

MELANIE. Ego, coming from the man who watched the Tour de France once and now thinks he's Bradley Wiggins. /

SAM. I'll get one to examine your cough whilst I'm at it, should I?

BEN. / Queen of Sheeba expecting the world to revolve around you. /

RACHEL. I don't have a cough!

BEN. / Seven months, you've not contributed one thing to this flat. No tea, no toilet roll, no washing-up liquid /

SAM. Yes you do – throughout intercourse.

MELANIE. / But nothing could be further from the truth. Wiggins, he was dedicated, had a life plan /

RACHEL. How do you know that?

SAM. Because I listened!

BEN. / nothing, apart from the desperate smell of a thirty-two-year-old who knows her ovaries are rotting /

RACHEL. Why are you listening to us having sex, you pervert?! Deviant! /

MELANIE. / whereas you, you're just a lazy tosser on an undersized bike with a haircut!

SAM. Cough. Cough. Cough. /

BEN. / and her level of attraction is falling at the same rate as her tits!

RACHEL. / Stop making that noise! Stop it!!

BEN. Hear that, Mel, hear that?!

SAM. / Cough. Cough!

MELANIE. You horrid cretin.

RACHEL. Well, you're just a rebound. A rebound, that's all you are, Sam!

MELANIE. Ignore her, Sam, she's just jealous /

RACHEL. Of wonky-anus man, I don't think so!!

MELANIE. / because you will achieve more in a week than Ben will ever do in his life!

RACHEL. Get out of my sight. Get out!!

MELANIE. This is our room!!

RACHEL. Get out!!!

MELANIE. No, you get out!!

RACHEL. I can't look at you!!

MELANIE. Then go to your own fucking room!!

RACHEL. I will!!!

> RACHEL *turns and goes to her room.* BEN *follows.* RACHEL *tries to compose herself. During the following she finds the contract. She stares at it. A moment.*

MELANIE. Rach. Rach? Rach?! Ben. Please. I'm. Please…

SAM. Melanie. We have to get the contract witnessed, don't we? Dr Parsons shift change will be taking place soon. So we have to go. Let's get the file. Yes?

> *Eventually* MELANIE *goes to the living room. Gets the file.*

RACHEL. This isn't fair.

BEN. No.

RACHEL. They don't live here.

> RACHEL *tears up the contract.*

BEN. What are you doing?

RACHEL. You just agree with me.

BEN. Erm…

RACHEL *walks out of the bedroom,* BEN *follows her.*

RACHEL. Where are you planning on staying till you complete?

SAM. Pardon?

RACHEL. It's a straightforward question.

MELANIE. Here.

RACHEL. Do you live here?

SAM. Well, this is our room.

RACHEL. Is it?

SAM. Those are our clothes.

RACHEL. Funny, it looks different to me. Does it to you, Ben?

BEN. Yes.

RACHEL. Does it look like our living room?

BEN. It does, yes.

MELANIE. What you talking about?

RACHEL. How much are hotels in London? Expensive aren't they, of course they are, it's London. Six weeks to complete. That's optimistically speaking.

BEN. Very optimistic.

RACHEL. I'm sure there are a few sofas you can crash on in the short term. Here and there. But what if it drags on? Goodwill soon fades. And then those hotel visits get pricey. And then what if it falls through, if that happens?

MELANIE. What are you saying?

RACHEL. I'm saying that you don't live here. That there's no record of you living here. There's no contract, is there, Sam? No reference to a deposit. You're just guests. And there comes a point where guests are no longer welcome.

SAM. You'll return our deposit.

RACHEL. No, we won't.

SAM. Then you won't get any more rent from us.

RACHEL. So be it. From now on, every penny we have ever put aside will get eaten up, lost, to cover the rent we can't afford.

BEN. Rach...?

RACHEL. But we will do it. If you think I could live with you both.

MELANIE. I'm not hearing Rachel right now, I don't know who I'm hearing. Stop and think about what you're saying.

RACHEL. You need a document to be signed? I'm guessing it needs to be witnessed. And I'm guessing you need that now to process your sale. You better go then. But just know that by the time you return, your belongings will have been packed up and left outside. Won't they, Ben.

BEN. Yes.

RACHEL. The locks will be double-bolted and I will happily pay for them all to be changed. This is over. Do you hear that, Mel?

MELANIE. Fifteen years we've been friends.

RACHEL. Just a chapter, though, really. In the scheme of things, right. Do you need a pen? For the contracts? Here. It's the least we can do really after how much you've helped us out. After all, we're all in this together, aren't we.

Stalemate.

SAM and MELANIE move out. RACHEL and BEN stare at the space. RACHEL and BEN go to different rooms. They argue.

July

BEN *and* RACHEL. BEN *is wearing a very nice coat.*

RACHEL. How much?

BEN. You've got the receipt there, you can see exactly how much.

RACHEL. Say it out loud.

BEN. Why? I was completely sane when I was buying it.

RACHEL. Five hundred pounds!

BEN. Yes.

RACHEL. Five hundred pounds.

BEN. It won't change the more you say it.

RACHEL. Your entire wardrobe combined doesn't cost that much! Don't walk away from me.

BEN. Why not, we've got all this extra space I might as well make use of it.

RACHEL. Five hundred fucking pounds!

BEN. I saw it and I wanted it so I got it.

RACHEL. I'm so happy for you, that's so lovely.

BEN. Sarcasm is not something you're really au fait with, Rach, I'd recommend sticking with shouting the number out like a parrot.

RACHEL. Can't even just say 'fuck off', can you.

BEN. Fuck off.

RACHEL. That's over a third of the rent.

BEN. I can do the maths.

RACHEL. How did you pay for it?

BEN. With my money.

RACHEL. Your money?

BEN. What do you want to hear, from our joint account? Yes. There.

RACHEL. That's our money.

BEN. I'll put the money in when I get paid.

RACHEL. The next rent comes out before you get paid.

BEN. Or from my savings then. But it is my money.

RACHEL. You held it against me for buying a top that was twenty pounds.

BEN. Well, that was then.

RACHEL. 'Then'?

BEN. When we weren't just throwing money away. When we were working together.

RACHEL. Oh don't go there again.

BEN. How can I not?

RACHEL. You agreed with me.

BEN. You said to just agree with you. And I did. Blindly. I nodded because I was there to support you. And when I was doing that you didn't think anything about me. You only thought about how much you were hurt. And that feeling you had has fucked us both over. Massively.

RACHEL. Yeah, yeah, that's so true. I was deeply, deeply hurt. But you can't, you can't hold that against me.

BEN. I do.

RACHEL. You've got to stop then because you let them walk out the door. You stood there and watched them go. Silently. You did that.

BEN *shows the price tag on the jacket.*

BEN. The tag's still on it.

RACHEL. Well take it back tomorrow.

BEN. Remember that cheque my parents gave me for my thirty-fifth? I put that into our savings account. I didn't buy myself anything. They were delighted to think it would help towards us getting on the ladder. Bless them, wouldn't even cover the cost of this coat, let alone get us a rung. And now to think that money they gave, with that hope, is just going to be thrown away, to line the pocket of some parasite, to… I'll take this back. But this, this scenario we can't. I don't know what we're doing, Rach.

RACHEL. I know.

BEN. It makes no sense.

RACHEL. I know.

BEN. I always thought that was something we had.

A moment.

This can't be our final chapter. Swallow your pride.

BEN *and* RACHEL *stare at each other. They move away from each other. They spend time in separate rooms.* BEN *goes.*

August

MELANIE *and* RACHEL.

MELANIE. I saw Ben on my way here. In The Florence.

RACHEL. Yeah.

MELANIE. I'd heard he was working there.

RACHEL. We need the extra cash. I'm marking exam papers. Tutoring. Anything that pays.

MELANIE. So you're managing? Coping?

RACHEL. What do you fucking think?

MELANIE. I can't keep apologising.

RACHEL. You could start though.

MELANIE. I'm sorry. I am so sorry, Rach.

RACHEL. Stop that, I've not asked you round for a hug.

MELANIE. Do you know that when I got your text I cried. I
    literally bawled my eyes out because I've missed you so much.

RACHEL. Are you saying this because it's fallen through?
    Because I really don't know what to believe when it comes
    out of your mouth any more.

MELANIE. It's true. I miss you. Massively. Have you missed
    me?

RACHEL. Don't kid yourself, I text you because of Ben. That's
    why you're here.

MELANIE. That's not true, is it.

RACHEL. What happened to your flat?

MELANIE. We got gazumped. You're allowed to smile.

RACHEL. Why would I smile? Have you run out of places to
    stay?

MELANIE. Yes.

RACHEL. So that's why you came running.

MELANIE. I'm just being honest. The way we should have
    been from the start. We weren't and that was totally wrong.
    We, I, made a mistake, a massive one. And so yes, full
    disclosure, right now we're stuck – we're no way near buying
    anything, so we'd have to rent something for a minimum of
    a year and we can't do that. But it's not just that, we want to
    come back. To make things right. We got into this together as
    friends. We should end this together as friends.

RACHEL. Sam sees it the same way, does he?

MELANIE. Of course he does. Please, Rach, please don't hurt
    yourselves to prove a point. We all need this.

RACHEL. I don't know if I can forget what you did.

MELANIE. I know you. I know you will be able to. You're too
    good a person.

Time passes. MELANIE *and* SAM *move back in.* BEN *and* RACHEL *watch them.*

Hi.

SAM. Hi.

BEN. Hello.

MELANIE. Oh, I bet you get a great view from that window. Yes, you do, look you can see The Shard if you lean out. Hear that, Sam?

SAM. Yes.

MELANIE. The Shard.

SAM. Yes.

MELANIE. Great view. Really panoramic.

BEN. I'll leave you to it.

SAM. Okay.

MELANIE. Sure. Yes. We don't need a tour.

RACHEL. No.

MELANIE. We know where everything is.

RACHEL. Yes.

Time passes. They move like robots around the house, avoiding each other.

September

The bedroom. BEN *and* RACHEL *argue. Meanwhile, in the living room,* SAM *tries to sleep.*

RACHEL. You've been drinking.

BEN. I stopped by the pub on my way home.

RACHEL. Hanging round, drinking with teenagers again.

BEN. Not all teenagers. Most are graduates can't even get a –

RACHEL. Whatever they are.

BEN. You should try it.

RACHEL. Should I?

    MELANIE *enters the flat, she can't help but overhear.*

BEN. Great for perspective.

RACHEL. Perspective?!

BEN. Yeah, think we're fucked.

RACHEL. I do think we're fucked.

BEN. I meant like as a generation, they're even more seriously screwed. Bigger debt, expected to work for free –

RACHEL. Stop pretending you're noble, you're not some social commentator, you're just being a prick hiding from his girlfriend.

BEN. You know, I thought when they moved back in that we'd be okay, we'd find our way back to each other, but it's not true, as now, when I think of you, I still think stupid –

RACHEL. What?

BEN. …. Stupid… fu…

RACHEL. If you let it out of your mouth it's out there.

BEN. I know.

RACHEL. You can't take it back.

BEN. Do you want me to say it?

RACHEL. I don't want you to speak.

BEN. I don't want to speak either. But I'm scared I will.

RACHEL. So go then.

BEN *goes.* MELANIE *has crept into the living room, where* SAM *is attempting to sleep.*

MELANIE. Sam? Wake up.

SAM. I have a shift in two hours, I need to sleep.

MELANIE. I had a voicemail from an estate agent today. Have you instructed them to search again for us? Sam?

SAM. Should I not have?

MELANIE. Didn't you think to mention it to me?

SAM. Have things changed?

MELANIE. Part of me goes, I don't know if I can go through all that rigmarole again. Sam? Don't turn away from me.

SAM. I need to go to sleep, Melanie.

A moment, then MELANIE *goes to the place where she could always find comfort:* RACHEL, *who is in the bedroom.*

MELANIE. Hi.

RACHEL. Hi.

MELANIE. Good day?

RACHEL. I've got marking to do.

MELANIE. Of course, yes, yes marking. Are you okay? Rach. The walls are so thin here, aren't they. Paper.

RACHEL. Spit it out, Mel.

MELANIE. I heard. You and Ben. I didn't know you two spoke to each other like that. So much spite.

RACHEL. Well, we do.

MELANIE. You've got to stay strong, you know, both of you.

RACHEL. Do we?

MELANIE. Of course, you're a constant, you've got roots. If you two fall apart –

RACHEL. What hope for you?

MELANIE. That's not what I mean.

RACHEL. But.

MELANIE. Sam and I are nothing compared to you, I know that. He doesn't talk to me any more. Not that he ever really has but since this –

RACHEL. Stop. Stop it. Whatever you think I am: a confidante, a friend, that memory – it's gone.

MELANIE. No, no, that's not true.

RACHEL. It is.

MELANIE. We will move on from this. We will have this as a blip in our history. When we're looking back from the comfort of our own homes and –

RACHEL. You really think that's still going to happen? Wake up, Mel. Wake up.

MELANIE *doesn't know what to do. She goes to her room. Sits on the edge of the bed by* SAM, *who never turns to acknowledge her. Time passes. Wind and rain batter the building. Leaks form. Drips fall.*

October

SAM *is placing bowls, buckets to catch the drips*. RACHEL *watches on*.

SAM. You'll have to call the estate agent. It's your responsibility to inform them of any issues such as this. If you don't, you'll be held accountable for any damage.

RACHEL. I don't care. Let it rot. Let it cave in, I don't care.

SAM. That's not what you think.

RACHEL. Don't presume to tell me what I'm thinking.

SAM. It's your foot you're shooting yourself in.

RACHEL. Then let me pull the trigger.

SAM. Something is wrong.

RACHEL. Something? That's the word you're choosing to use?

SAM. If you require someone to talk to, should you wish, you can talk to me.

RACHEL. You?

SAM. Shout. Cry. Unburden. I won't respond.

Surprised by herself, RACHEL *takes the offer.*

RACHEL. I got called a name today I haven't been called in years. In fact, not since I came to London. It was a seven-year-old. Seven years old. If this is how it's going, if that's how people are going to start talking to me *here*, in London, where I thought I was safe, then why should I even fight to stay? Ben didn't even answer the phone when I called him to talk. Rang and rang. And now in my head, all I'm thinking is if Ben was more ambitious we'd never be in this situation. I fell in love with a man who I thought could do anything.

SAM. Rachel.

RACHEL. You said you wouldn't respond.

SAM. It's important you know that the first time we played chess – Ben nearly beat me.

RACHEL *can't help but smile.*

RACHEL. Sam, why did you come back? You could have easily found somewhere else to live.

SAM. We had an obligation.

RACHEL. Oh, don't try to be honourable, that ship sailed a long, long time ago.

SAM. I'm a rebound. You said that to me.

RACHEL. I did, yes.

SAM. I've never had that taken back.

RACHEL. We all said things in the heat of the moment, but I can't take that back.

SAM. I wanted Melanie and I to rent a new flat. The two of us. Rather than return here. Yet still she insisted we came back. Here. To this. To you.

RACHEL. What do you want, Sam? From all of this, from her?

SAM. Very little. Very little.

RACHEL. I'm sorry.

They continue to watch the water drip. Time passes. Chunks of plaster give way. BEN rushes in, he finds RACHEL in the bedroom. SAM is in the living room.

I've been calling you.

BEN. Yes, I know. We have to talk.

RACHEL. Yes, we do.

BEN. Rachel.

RACHEL. Rachel??!!

BEN. Look, it's been a crazy day /

RACHEL. Yes, it has.

BEN. / they've offered me redundancy –

RACHEL. What?

BEN. Yeah. Voluntary. Cuts are being made. And I'm going to take it.

RACHEL. Oh are you?

BEN. Yes.

RACHEL. This isn't something you just decide.

BEN. Rach, I'm doing it for us.

RACHEL. Us?

BEN. It's a great deal, the money it could help us start again –

RACHEL. Are you mad?

BEN. No, no I'm not mad, I'm just, I'm average. Just completely average.

RACHEL. Oh fuck off, don't paint me a sob story.

BEN. I'm not, I promise.

RACHEL. Yes you are. '*Average*', all I'm hearing is me, me, me.

BEN. Yes, you're right, you're completely right. I've started this wrong, it's just, Rach, what I'm trying to say is that there's only one thing that's not average about me.

RACHEL. Is that right?

BEN. Yeah it is. And that's you. And what we have.

RACHEL. Are you kidding me?! This isn't *Love Actually*.

BEN. Rach, it's true though, this is something I am so blessed with, something that everyone searches for –

RACHEL. You think people want this?

BEN. Of course I do.

MELANIE *enters the flat. Slowly and wearily she goes to join* SAM *in the living room.*

I'm sorry I didn't answer your calls.

RACHEL. You think it's just about a phone call?!

BEN. Rach –

RACHEL. We can't survive like this.

BEN. No, no we can't, that's why we have to leave.

RACHEL. Sorry? Leave?

MELANIE. Hi.

BEN. Here. London.

SAM. Hello.

BEN. We could start living again. Build a new future.

> MELANIE *goes to the kitchen, drinks a glass of water. She lingers.*

RACHEL. Oh we will, will we?

BEN. No, no, Rach, I don't mean to demand that, I mean, what I hope, I hope so so much you still want that. I will go wherever you want: Bristol, Manchester, Sheffield, Cardiff, Liverpool –

RACHEL. Stop just naming cities.

BEN. I mean it though, if I take redundancy then I will happily do any job, I don't care, I'll do anything if I can come home to you.

RACHEL. We can't do that.

BEN. We can. We can start afresh. Remember what we were like before this began? Everything we dreamt of. We could make that happen elsewhere.

RACHEL. What if it's not this place, what if it's just you and me that's gone to shit and we should just call it a day?

> MELANIE *has rejoined* SAM *in the living room.*

MELANIE. I'm not happy.

SAM. I know.

BEN. You don't believe that. Do you, Rach?

MELANIE. You're not happy.

SAM. No.

BEN. Look, I know I've not been who you needed, that I've let you and myself down, but I'm going to change. I know what's important now. It's so clear. And that's you. Rach, it's you. It's us. We can't lose that.

MELANIE. I think we should stop this.

RACHEL. I don't want to flee.

SAM. Okay.

BEN. It's not fleeing.

RACHEL. It is.

MELANIE. That's all I'm going to get?

BEN. We have given it our best, haven't we.

SAM. Yes.

BEN. We have given this city more chances than it deserves and it doesn't feel the same back.

MELANIE. You're not going to fight for us?

BEN. It doesn't want us. It doesn't protect us. And that's a tragedy for it, not us.

RACHEL. But London is our home.

SAM. Why?

BEN. It's not our home.

SAM. You know this isn't right.

BEN. A home is a place you want to come home to. A home is a place you feel happy in. A home is a place you build together.

SAM. I know what I am to you.

BEN. Rach?

SAM. It's not your fault.

RACHEL. What if it's not any better in any of those places?

BEN. We've got to give ourselves the chance to find out.

SAM. We both deserve better.

RACHEL. Ben, what if it's just as hard?

BEN. Then at least we'll still have each other, won't we.
    Won't we?

RACHEL. I've been in love with you for nearly half my life.

MELANIE. Sam.

RACHEL. Ben... I...

BEN. No, Rach... no...

SAM. You'll be absolutely fine, Melanie.

RACHEL. I don't think you're average.

BEN. That's all that matters to me.

MELANIE. And so will you?

BEN. Is that a yes?

RACHEL *and* SAM. Yes.

> SAM *goes as* RACHEL *and* BEN *embrace*. MELANIE
> *watches on*. RACHEL *sits with* MELANIE. MELANIE
> *leans into* RACHEL. RACHEL *lets her. Their year ends*.
> *They pack up their belongings*.

November

The living room. MELANIE *waits for* BEN *and* RACHEL.

MELANIE. So that's me all ready.

RACHEL. Yes.

BEN. You've ordered a taxi?

MELANIE. It will be here shortly. Take me straight to the new flat. My new roomie. And you?

BEN. The van.

MELANIE. Course, yes, totally. And you're going to drive there today?

BEN. After the inventory.

MELANIE. Inventory, yes. Oh god, look at this place. Weird, sofa there.

BEN. Yeah.

MELANIE. I wonder who is going to move in? Bet they sold it on the views. Properly panoramic. The Shard. Hear that?

RACHEL. Yes.

MELANIE. The Shard, you can see it. Do you remember all the tears when we left halls?

RACHEL. I do, yes.

MELANIE. Drama queens.

Beep of a car horn.

That will be…

BEN. The taxi.

MELANIE. Yes. I'm really excited for you both. Bristol! Let me know when you arrive. Send me pictures. And we'll have to sort out a visit. Obviously when you're settled. And…

Another beep.

BEN. Probably blocking the road.

MELANIE. I better go then…

RACHEL. Yeah.

BEN. You're going to have a great time, Mel, you know that.

MELANIE. Yeah. Thirty-three and single, time to mingle.

BEN. You're in a good place.

MELANIE. Yeah. Totally. I know. Yes.

BEN. Goodbye, Mel.

MELANIE. Bye, Ben. Bye, Rach.

RACHEL. Goodbye.

> MELANIE *goes*. RACHEL *and* BEN *remain*.
>
> *The sun pours through the window.*
>
> *End.*

www.nickhernbooks.co.uk

facebook.com/nickhernbooks

twitter.com/nickhernbooks